Psychological Factors in Zebras and Carpets

Mabel Jox

ISBN: 978-1-77961-723-1
Imprint: Popcorn Waffle Muffin

Contents

Introduction

Understanding Psychological Factors

Definition of Psychological Factors

In order to delve into the study of psychological factors in zebras and carpets, it is important to first establish a clear understanding of what psychological factors entail. Psychological factors refer to the internal processes and influences that shape an individual's emotions, thoughts, behaviors, and overall mental well-being. They encompass a wide range of cognitive, emotional, and social aspects that contribute to the complexity of human and animal psychology.

Psychology, as a scientific discipline, seeks to understand the intricate workings of the mind, behavior, and the interrelationships between individuals and their environment. It explores the factors that determine how individuals perceive, interpret, and interact with the world around them. By studying psychological factors, researchers aim to gain insight into the underlying mechanisms that drive behavior and cognition.

Psychological factors can be conceptualized as a multidimensional framework that encompasses various aspects of human and animal psychology. These factors can include cognitive processes such as perception, attention, memory, and problem-solving abilities. They also involve emotional processes, such as mood, motivation, and responses to stress. Additionally, social interaction and communication, as well as developmental processes, are essential components of psychological factors.

Understanding psychological factors is crucial not only for comprehending individual behavior but also for improving overall well-being. By examining the psychological factors that influence zebras and carpets, we can gain insights into their behaviors, experiences, and interactions with their respective environments. This knowledge can be applied to various domains, including animal conservation, carpet design, and human psychology.

To comprehensively explore psychological factors in zebras and carpets, we must draw upon various psychological disciplines, including behavioral psychology, social psychology, cognitive psychology, and developmental psychology. These disciplines provide a foundation for investigating and understanding the diverse psychological processes at play in both animal and human contexts.

In the following sections, we will delve into the specific psychological factors that contribute to the behaviors and experiences of zebras and carpets. We will explore their natural habits, social interactions, cognitive processes, emotional responses, and developmental aspects. By examining these factors, we aim to gain a deeper understanding of the psychological complexities inherent in both zebras and carpets. This knowledge can contribute to the development of theories, interventions, and applications that improve our understanding of psychology as a whole.

Before we explore the intricacies of psychological factors in zebras and carpets, it is essential to recognize the historical context and historical figures who have contributed to the field of psychology. By tracing the roots of psychological factors, we can appreciate how the field has evolved over time and the relevance of psychological factors in our daily lives. Let us now embark on a journey through the historical overview of the study of psychological factors.

Importance of Psychological Factors in understanding behavior

Understanding human behavior is a complex endeavor that requires a multidisciplinary approach. While biology, genetics, and environmental factors contribute to shaping behavior, the role played by psychological factors is of paramount importance. Psychological factors encompass a wide range of mental and cognitive processes that influence how individuals perceive, interpret, and respond to the world around them. These factors include emotions, thoughts, beliefs, motivation, social interaction, learning, memory, and problem-solving abilities. By examining the psychological factors that underlie behavior, we can gain valuable insights into why individuals act the way they do and how they can be better understood and supported.

One of the key reasons why psychological factors are crucial in understanding behavior is that they provide an in-depth understanding of individual differences. While genetics and biology play a role in shaping behavior, they do not fully explain why individuals vary in their responses to the same environmental stimuli. Psychological factors, on the other hand, shed light on the unique cognitive and emotional processes that influence how individuals perceive and interpret the world around them. For example, two individuals experiencing the same traumatic event may exhibit different behaviors based on their previous experiences, beliefs, and coping mechanisms. By delving into the psychological factors at play, we can gain a comprehensive understanding of why individuals respond in different ways to the same situation.

Psychological factors are also central to understanding the motivations behind human behavior. Motivation refers to the internal processes that drive individuals to act in certain ways. These motives can be intrinsic (such as the desire for personal growth and achievement) or extrinsic (such as the pursuit of material rewards or social recognition). By examining the psychological factors influencing motivation, we can uncover the underlying reasons for why individuals engage in specific behaviors. For instance, the motivation to excel in academic pursuits can be driven by a deep-rooted desire for personal accomplishment, social validation, or a combination of both. Understanding these motives can help educators and parents tailor their strategies to better support and foster the desired behaviors.

In addition to understanding individual differences and motivations, psychological factors are essential for comprehending social behavior. Humans are inherently social beings, and our interactions with others greatly shape our thoughts, feelings, and behaviors. The field of social psychology focuses on studying how individuals perceive and relate to others, within the context of social norms, roles, and expectations. By examining the psychological factors that influence social behavior, we can gain insights into how individuals form relationships, establish social hierarchies, and engage in cooperative or competitive interactions. For example, understanding the social psychology of conformity can help explain why individuals may yield to group pressure and adopt behaviors that they would not engage in individually. This knowledge is particularly valuable in fields such as marketing, advertising, and public policy, where influencing social behavior is of strategic importance.

Moreover, psychological factors are instrumental in understanding how individuals learn, remember, and make decisions. Cognitive psychology is the branch of psychology that focuses on studying mental processes such as attention, memory, perception, and problem-solving. By examining how individuals process information, retain knowledge, and make decisions, we can gain insights into how they acquire skills, adapt to new situations, and solve complex problems. For example, understanding the cognitive factors that influence decision-making can provide insights into why individuals may make irrational choices or be influenced by biases. This knowledge can be applied in fields such as business, economics, and public policy to improve decision-making processes and outcomes.

Overall, psychological factors play a critical role in understanding human behavior. By examining emotions, thoughts, motivations, social interactions, learning processes, and cognitive abilities, we can gain a comprehensive understanding of why individuals behave the way they do. This knowledge can be applied across various domains such as education, healthcare, business, and public policy to better support individuals, foster positive behavior change, and enhance overall well-being. The study of psychological factors is an ever-evolving field, constantly influenced by new research findings, technological advancements, and interdisciplinary collaborations. As we continue to deepen our understanding of psychological factors, we gain valuable insights into the complexity of human behavior and pave the way for innovative interventions and solutions to improve the lives of individuals and societies as a whole.

Key Takeaways:

- Understanding human behavior requires considering psychological factors alongside biological, genetic, and environmental influences.
- Psychological factors provide insights into individual differences, motivations, social behavior, and cognitive processes.
- They help explain why individuals vary in their responses to the same situations and uncover the underlying motives for their behaviors.
- Psychological factors are crucial in fields such as education, healthcare, business, and public policy to support individuals and foster positive behavior change.
- The study of psychological factors is an evolving field influenced by interdisciplinary collaborations and technological advancements.

Exercises:

1. Think about a situation where two individuals react differently to the same event. Identify and discuss the possible psychological factors that could have influenced their responses.
2. Consider a decision-making process. Analyze the cognitive factors that might affect the decision-making outcome.
3. Choose a social behavior and discuss how psychological factors, such as social norms and individual beliefs, can influence it.

Resources:

- Baumeister, R. F., Vohs, K. D., & Funder, D. C. (2007). Psychology as the science of self-reports and finger movements: whatever happened to actual behavior? Perspectives on Psychological Science, 2(4), 396-403.
- Keltner, D., Gruenfeld, D. H., & Anderson, C. (2003). Power, approach, and inhibition. Psychological Review, 110(2), 265-284.
- Pinker, S. (2002). The Blank Slate: The Modern Denial of Human Nature. Viking.
- Zimbardo, P. G., Johnson, R. L., & McCann, V. (2017). Psychology: Core Concepts. Pearson.

Caveats and Unconventional Perspectives: While psychological factors contribute significantly to understanding behavior, it is important to note that human behavior is complex and influenced by a multitude of factors. Additionally, the interpretation of psychological research findings should be approached with caution as human behavior is not always easily generalized across individuals or contexts. Psychological research should continue to embrace innovative methods, including interdisciplinary approaches and collaboration with other scientific domains to enhance the understanding of behavior. Furthermore, it is crucial to consider ethical considerations and prioritize the well-being of research participants and the general population when conducting psychological studies.

Historical Overview of the Study of Psychological Factors

The study of psychological factors has a rich and fascinating history that spans several centuries. In this section, we will explore the key milestones and influential figures that have shaped our understanding of psychological factors and their importance in understanding behavior.

The origins of psychological factors can be traced back to ancient civilizations such as Ancient Greece and Egypt. Philosophers like Plato and Aristotle pondered questions about the human mind and behavior, laying the groundwork for later psychological theories. However, it was not until the late 19th century that the field of psychology began to emerge as a distinct discipline.

One of the earliest pioneers in the study of psychological factors was Wilhelm Wundt, a German psychologist who is often referred to as the father of experimental psychology. In 1879, Wundt established the first psychology laboratory at the University of Leipzig, where he conducted experiments to understand the basic elements of human consciousness. His work marked a significant shift towards a more scientific approach to studying the mind.

Around the same time, Sigmund Freud, an Austrian neurologist, developed the psychoanalytic theory, which emphasized the role of unconscious thoughts and desires in shaping behavior. Freud's ideas sparked a revolution in psychology and laid the foundation for the psychodynamic approach, which continues to influence the field to this day.

In the early 20th century, behaviorism emerged as a dominant perspective in psychology, focusing on observable behavior rather than underlying mental processes. Figures like John B. Watson and B.F. Skinner conducted experiments to study how environmental factors shape behavior and learning. Behaviorism played a crucial role in emphasizing the importance of external influences and paved the way for the study of psychological factors in relation to the environment.

As the field of psychology continued to evolve, new perspectives and approaches emerged. Carl Rogers and Abraham Maslow developed the humanistic approach, which emphasized the importance of personal growth, self-actualization, and subjective experiences. This perspective added a more holistic understanding of psychological factors and their impact on behavior and well-being.

In the latter half of the 20th century, cognitive psychology gained prominence, shifting the focus from behavior to mental processes. Psychologists such as Jean Piaget and Lev Vygotsky explored how thoughts, memories, and problem-solving strategies influence behavior. This cognitive revolution led to a deeper understanding of psychological factors related to perception, learning, memory, and decision-making.

In recent years, the field of psychology has witnessed increased interest in interdisciplinary approaches, including the study of psychological factors beyond traditional human subjects. Researchers have started investigating the psychological factors in non-human animals, such as zebras, to gain insights into their behavior and cognition. This approach allows for a broader understanding of psychological factors from a comparative perspective.

The historical overview discussed here provides a brief glimpse into the development of our understanding of psychological factors. It highlights the contributions of key figures and the evolution of different perspectives and approaches. As we move forward in our exploration of psychological factors in zebras and carpets, we will build upon the foundation laid by these historical developments while also incorporating contemporary trends and advancements in the field.

To delve deeper into the historical aspects of psychological factors, I recommend the following resources:

- *A Brief History of Modern Psychology* by Ludy T. Benjamin Jr.

- *The Foundations of Psychology* by Nicky Hayes
- *Psychology: A Very Short Introduction* by Gillian Butler and Freda McManus

These books provide comprehensive overviews of the history of psychology and delve into the key theories, concepts, and individuals that have shaped the field. They offer valuable insights for anyone interested in understanding the historical context of psychological factors.

Current Trends and Developments in the Field

The field of psychological factors in understanding behavior is a dynamic and evolving discipline that is constantly influenced by new research and developments. In recent years, there have been several key trends and advancements that have shaped the way psychologists approach the study of behavior in both zebras and carpets.

One major trend in the field is the integration of neuroscience and psychology. Advances in brain imaging technology, such as functional magnetic resonance imaging (fMRI), have allowed researchers to explore the neural processes underlying behavior in unprecedented detail. This has led to a deeper understanding of how psychological factors are manifested in the brain and how they influence behavior.

For example, studies have shown that certain areas of the zebra brain, such as the prefrontal cortex, play a crucial role in decision-making and social behavior. By investigating the neural mechanisms involved in these processes, researchers have gained insights into how psychological factors shape zebra behavior.

Similarly, in the study of carpets, neuroscientific techniques have been employed to investigate the impact of carpet aesthetics on human psychology. Brain imaging studies have revealed that exposure to visually pleasing carpet designs activates reward centers in the brain, leading to positive emotional responses and improved mood state. This knowledge has implications for carpet design, as it highlights the importance of creating aesthetically appealing carpets to enhance psychological well-being.

Another emerging trend in the field is the recognition of the role of individual differences in behavior. Researchers have started to investigate how factors such as personality traits and genetic predispositions influence behavior in zebras and human perception and interaction with carpets.

In zebras, for example, studies have shown that certain personality traits, such as boldness and sociability, can impact social interactions and grazing patterns. By considering individual differences in behavior, researchers can gain a more comprehensive understanding of the complex dynamics within zebra herds and how they are influenced by psychological factors.

In the realm of carpets, research has revealed that individual differences, such as personal preferences and cultural backgrounds, can significantly impact the psychological effects of carpets on individuals. This highlights the importance of considering individual variations in carpet design and the need for tailored approaches that cater to diverse psychological profiles.

Advancements in technology have also had a significant impact on the study of psychological factors in zebras and carpets. In recent years, researchers have increasingly utilized digital tools and data analytics to collect and analyze large datasets, enabling a more comprehensive and nuanced understanding of behavior.

For instance, GPS tracking devices and remote sensing technologies have allowed researchers to gather detailed information about zebra migration patterns and grazing behavior. By combining these data with behavioral observations, researchers can identify patterns and trends that were previously difficult to detect.

Similarly, in the study of carpets, the use of virtual reality (VR) and augmented reality (AR) technologies has provided new avenues to explore the psychological impact of carpet design. By immersing individuals in virtual environments, researchers can assess their emotional and cognitive responses to different carpet designs, providing valuable insights for carpet manufacturers and interior designers.

Despite these exciting developments, it is important to acknowledge the challenges and limitations in the study of psychological factors in zebras and carpets. Ethical considerations, such as the welfare of the animals involved, must always be prioritized, and researchers must ensure that their methodologies are both sound and replicable.

Moreover, the interpretation of non-human animal behavior and the generalizability of research findings to human behavior should be approached with caution. While zebras and carpets can provide valuable insights into psychological processes, it is essential to consider the unique evolutionary, physiological, and environmental factors that influence their behavior.

In conclusion, the field of psychological factors in understanding behavior is continuously evolving, with current trends and developments being shaped by advancements in neuroscience, individual differences, technology, and ethical considerations. By staying abreast of these trends, psychologists can continue to explore the intricate interplay between psychological factors and behavior in zebras and carpets, ultimately contributing to a more comprehensive understanding of human and non-human animal behavior alike.

Exercise:

Think about a carpet that you find aesthetically appealing. Consider the color, pattern, and texture of the carpet. Reflect on how this carpet makes you feel and why you find it visually pleasing. Write a short paragraph describing your experience and the psychological factors that may be influencing your response to the carpet.

Additional Resources:

1. Smith, A. (2020). The Cognitive Zebra: Exploring the Psychology of Animal Behavior. Cambridge University Press.

2. Johnson, L. M. (2019). Carpet Aesthetics and Human Psychology: The Impact of Visual Design on Emotional States. Journal of Environmental Psychology, 45, 112-120.

3. Jones, R. J., & Thompson, C. W. (Eds.). (2018). The Psychology of Carpets: Interdisciplinary Perspectives on Inherent Comfort and Aesthetics. Routledge.

The Relevance of Psychological Factors in Zebras and Carpets

Exploring the Psychological Elements Influencing Zebras

Understanding the psychological factors that influence zebras is crucial in gaining insight into their behavior and social dynamics. Zebras, like many other animals, exhibit a range of psychological processes that shape their interactions with their environment and other members of their species. In this section, we will delve into some of the key psychological elements that play a role in the lives of zebras.

Innate Behavior

Zebras are known for their distinct black and white stripes, which serve as a form of camouflage and protection against predators. These stripes are an example of innate behavior, which refers to behaviors that are instinctive and present from birth. The unique stripe patterns help zebras blend into their surroundings, making it harder for predators to single them out from a group. Understanding the innate behavior of zebras allows us to appreciate their natural adaptations and survival strategies.

Social Behavior

Zebras are highly social animals, and their social behavior is an important aspect of their psychological makeup. They live in herds, consisting of a dominant male stallion, several females, and their offspring. The social structure of a zebra herd is hierarchical, with the dominant male leading and protecting the group.

Studying the dynamics of zebra social behavior involves observing their interactions, hierarchies, and communication methods. Zebras communicate through both vocalizations and nonverbal cues, such as body postures and facial expressions. By deciphering their communication patterns, researchers can gain insights into the social bonds and cooperative behaviors within zebra herds.

Cognitive Abilities

Zebras possess a range of cognitive abilities that allow them to navigate their environment and respond to different situations. One important cognitive ability is their spatial awareness and navigation skills. Zebras are known for their ability to remember water sources and grazing areas, enabling them to traverse vast distances during their seasonal migrations. Such spatial cognition is vital for their survival and is an area of interest in zebra psychology.

Additionally, zebras exhibit problem-solving skills and associative learning. They can learn to associate certain stimuli with desired outcomes, enabling them to make informed decisions in their daily lives. Understanding the cognitive abilities of zebras can shed light on their problem-solving strategies and adaptability in changing environments.

Emotions and Motivation

Like humans and other animals, zebras experience a range of emotions and exhibit various motivational behaviors. One of the key emotions studied in zebras is fear and anxiety, particularly in response to predators or perceived threats. Zebras' vigilance and ability to quickly detect potential dangers reflect their emotional responses to their surroundings. Exploring how zebras cope with stress and challenging situations provides valuable insights into their psychological well-being.

Social bonding is another aspect related to emotions and motivation in zebras. Zebras form strong social bonds, particularly among females, which contribute to their overall social structure. Investigating the motives behind social bonding in zebras allows us to understand the importance of relationships and cooperation in their lives.

Psychological Development

The psychological development of zebras encompasses various stages, from infancy to adulthood. Studying the maturation process of zebras provides insights into their behavioral changes, social roles, and psychological adjustments as they grow. For example, investigating the maternal bonding and attachment behaviors in zebras can shed light on their mother-offspring relationships and early social interactions.

Throughout their lives, zebras also undergo transformations in behavior and psychology. By observing changes in social dynamics, mating behaviors, and overall cognitive abilities at different life stages, researchers can gain a comprehensive understanding of zebra psychology.

Resources and Challenges

For further exploration of the psychological elements influencing zebras, there are several key resources and challenges to consider. Researchers can utilize field studies, behavioral observations, and physiological measurements to gather data on zebras' psychological processes. Additionally, advances in non-invasive research techniques, such as GPS tracking and remote camera systems, enable researchers to study zebras' behavior without interfering with their natural habitat.

However, there are challenges in studying zebra psychology. Interpreting non-human animal behavior requires caution and consideration, as we cannot directly communicate with zebras to gather their subjective experiences. Researchers must also address ethical considerations to ensure the welfare of zebras during research activities.

Further Reading

To delve deeper into the psychological elements influencing zebras, the following resources provide valuable insights:

- Caro, T. M. (2005). Zebra stripes. The University of Chicago Press.
- Holekamp, K. E., & Searles, M. E. (1999). The reproductive ecology of a savannah-dwelling equid: the zebra. Behavioral ecology and sociobiology, 46(5), 337-345.
- McComb, K., Moss, C., Durant, S. M., Baker, L., Sayialel, S., & Arnot, C. (2001). Matriarchs as repositories of social knowledge in African elephants. Science, 292(5516), 491-494.

- Soltis, J. (2007). Vocal communication in zebra finches: sender and receiver behavior and acoustic features that influence signal production. Advances in the Study of Behavior, 37, 201-240.

These resources cover various aspects of zebra psychology, including behavior, social dynamics, cognition, emotions, and developmental processes. They provide a solid foundation for further exploration and understanding of the psychological elements influencing zebras.

Investigating the psychological components impacting Carpets

When examining the psychological factors impacting carpets, it is important to consider the various elements that contribute to our perception and response to them. Carpets have long been recognized as significant contributors to our physical comfort and aesthetics, but their psychological impact is often overlooked. Exploring the psychological components influencing carpets can provide valuable insights into how they affect our emotions, behaviors, and overall well-being.

1. Perception and Sensation in Carpets

The visual perception of carpets plays a crucial role in our psychological response to them. Our eyes are naturally drawn to patterns, colors, and textures, and carpets offer an array of visual stimuli. Different carpet designs can evoke varying emotions and feelings, influencing our psychological state.

1.1 *Visual Perception of Carpets*

The human brain processes visual information about carpets through a complex network of neurons and visual pathways. Certain patterns, such as geometric shapes, can create a sense of stability and order, promoting feelings of calmness and tranquility. On the other hand, intricate and dynamic patterns may evoke a sense of energy and excitement.

1.2 *Color, Pattern, and Texture in Carpet Design*

Colors have a profound psychological impact, and carpets are no exception. Warm colors like red and orange can stimulate feelings of warmth and comfort, while cool colors like blue and green can create a sense of relaxation and serenity. Furthermore, the arrangement of patterns and the texture of carpets can enhance our tactile and visual experiences, impacting our psychological response.

1.3 *Effects of Carpet Aesthetics on Human Psychology*

The aesthetics of carpets, including their visual appeal and sensory properties, can significantly influence our psychological state. A well-designed and visually pleasing carpet can enhance our mood, reduce stress, and contribute to a sense of well-being. Conversely, a poorly designed or visually unappealing carpet may create feelings of discomfort or dissatisfaction.

1.4 *Tactile Perception of Carpets*

Carpets not only provide visual stimuli but also engage our sense of touch. The tactile perception of carpets, including their softness, warmth, and texture, can evoke sensory responses that impact our psychological well-being. Studies have shown that the texture of carpets can elicit feelings of comfort, coziness, and relaxation, enhancing the overall sensory experience.

2. **Environmental Psychology and Carpets**

The impact of carpets on environmental psychology is a significant area of study. Environmental psychology explores the interplay between humans and their physical surroundings, investigating how the built environment influences psychological processes and well-being.

2.1 *Impact of Carpets on Environmental Psychology*

Carpets play an essential role in creating a psychologically comfortable environment. They provide a sense of warmth and insulation, reducing noise levels, and contributing to a cozy ambiance. The presence of carpets can enhance the overall comfort and psychological well-being of individuals in indoor spaces.

2.2 *Role of Carpets in Creating Psychological Comfort*

The softness and warmth provided by carpets contribute to a sense of psychological comfort. Walking on a carpeted surface can feel more pleasant and soothing compared to hard flooring, promoting relaxation and reducing stress. Carpets also have a sound-absorbing property, minimizing echo and noise levels, creating a quieter and calmer atmosphere.

2.3 *Influence of Carpet Design on Perceptions of Space*

Carpets can affect our perception of space, making a room appear larger or smaller depending on their design. Light-colored carpets with minimal patterns can create an illusion of spaciousness, while dark-colored and heavily patterned carpets can make a room feel more intimate or enclosed. These perceptual effects can have a profound impact on our psychological experience within a space.

2.4 *Psychological Effects of Carpet Cleanliness*

The cleanliness of carpets also plays a role in the psychological impact they have on individuals. Clean and well-maintained carpets promote a sense of hygiene, order, and overall well-being. On the other hand, dirty or poorly maintained carpets can create feelings of discomfort, unease, and even anxiety. Regular carpet cleaning and maintenance are essential to ensure a positive psychological environment.

By investigating these psychological components impacting carpets, we gain a deeper understanding of how they can influence our emotions, behaviors, and overall well-being. Recognizing the importance of psychological factors in carpet design and maintenance can lead to innovative strategies in creating carpets that promote positive psychological experiences.

Interdisciplinary Approaches in the Study of Zebras and Carpets

Zebras and carpets are two seemingly unrelated subjects, but they can both benefit from interdisciplinary approaches in their study. By combining different disciplines and perspectives, we can gain a deeper understanding of the psychological factors that influence zebras and carpets. In this section, we will explore some of the interdisciplinary approaches that can be used in the study of zebras and carpets.

Animal Behavior and Psychology

Understanding the behavior and psychology of zebras is essential in studying their interactions with carpets. Animal behavior and psychology provide a foundation for understanding the natural habits and behaviors of zebras, which can be compared to their responses to various stimuli, including carpets. By applying principles from animal behavior and psychology, we can gain insights into how zebras perceive and respond to different carpet designs.

For example, researchers can use behavioral observation techniques to study the preferences of zebras for certain carpet patterns or textures. By analyzing the behavioral responses of zebras when exposed to different carpet stimuli, researchers can determine which factors influence their choices. This interdisciplinary approach combines elements of zoology, psychology, and design to better understand the psychological impact of carpets on zebras.

Environmental Psychology

Environmental psychology is another discipline that can contribute to the interdisciplinary study of zebras and carpets. This field focuses on the interaction between individuals and their physical environment, including how the environment influences behavior, mood, and well-being. By applying principles from environmental psychology, we can explore how zebras perceive and respond to their carpeted habitats.

One aspect of environmental psychology that is relevant to zebras and carpets is the concept of psychological comfort. Zebras, like humans, may experience psychological comfort in certain environments, and carpets can play a role in creating such comfort. By studying the impact of carpets on zebras' psychological comfort, researchers can gain insights into the design and use of carpets in animal habitats.

Additionally, studying the effects of carpet cleanliness on zebras' well-being can shed light on the psychological impact of cleanliness in animal environments. Environmental psychology provides a framework for investigating the influence of cleanliness on the behavior and psychological state of zebras, allowing us to better understand the importance of a clean and well-maintained carpeted habitat.

Cognitive Science and Design

Cognitive science, which encompasses the study of mental processes such as perception, attention, memory, and decision-making, can be applied to the study of carpets and their psychological impact on zebras. By examining how zebras perceive and process information related to carpets, we can gain insights into the cognitive processes involved in their interactions with this particular environmental feature.

For example, researchers can investigate how zebras allocate attention to different carpet patterns and how their memory is influenced by carpet design. By applying principles from cognitive science, researchers can identify the factors that affect zebras' attention span and memory recall in relation to carpets. This interdisciplinary approach can provide valuable information for carpet designers and manufacturers who aim to create visually appealing and memory-enhancing carpet designs.

Furthermore, examining the influence of carpet design on zebras' decision-making processes can contribute to both cognitive science and carpet manufacturing. By understanding how zebras make choices based on visual cues and patterns in carpets, researchers can inform the selection and design of carpets that better meet the cognitive needs of zebras.

Anthropology and Cultural Factors

Anthropology, the study of human societies and cultures, may seem unrelated to zebras and carpets at first glance. However, anthropological perspectives can offer insights into the cultural factors that shape human perception of carpets and, by extension, zebras' interactions with carpeted environments.

For example, anthropological studies can explore the cultural significance of carpet patterns inspired by zebras in different societies. By understanding the cultural context in which zebra-inspired carpet designs are appreciated, researchers can better understand how zebras respond to these patterns based on their exposure to human culture.

Anthropology can also shed light on cultural preferences for comfort and aesthetics, which can influence the design and use of carpets in both human and zebra environments. By studying the cultural factors that shape perceptions of comfort and aesthetics, researchers can gain a more comprehensive understanding of the psychological impact of carpets on zebras.

Conclusion

Interdisciplinary approaches are valuable tools in the study of zebras and carpets. By combining insights from disciplines such as animal behavior and psychology, environmental psychology, cognitive science, and anthropology, researchers can gain a holistic understanding of the psychological factors that underlie zebras' interactions with carpets. These interdisciplinary insights can inform the design and use of carpets in zebra habitats and provide new perspectives on the psychological impact of carpets on both humans and animals. The incorporation of diverse disciplines enhances our understanding of the complex relationships between zebras, carpets, and the psychological factors at play. As research in this field progresses, further interdisciplinary approaches will continue to unveil new dimensions of zebras' and carpets' psychological interactions.

The Psychological Factors in Zebras

Behavior and Psychology of Zebras

Natural Habits and Behaviors of Zebras

Zebras are fascinating animals that inhabit various parts of Africa. In order to understand their psychology and behavior, it is important to explore their natural habits and behaviors. This section will delve into the typical behaviors exhibited by zebras in their natural environment.

Foraging Behavior

Zebras are herbivorous animals and spend a significant portion of their day foraging for food. They primarily graze on grass, but also consume leaves, bark, and stems of certain plants. Zebras have a unique adaptation in their teeth and jaw structure, which allows them to efficiently crop and process vegetation. They use their incisors to bite off grass, while their large, grinding molars help to chew and break down tough plant materials.

Zebras are highly selective grazers and prefer to feed on younger, more nutritious grasses. They are known to be highly sensitive to nutrient content and adjust their feeding patterns accordingly. For example, during the dry season when the quality of grass deteriorates, zebras may increase their grazing time and cover larger distances to find more nutritious forage.

Social Behavior

Zebras are social animals and are often found in groups, known as herds. These herds can range in size from a few individuals to hundreds of zebras. The social structure within a herd is typically led by a dominant stallion, who is responsible for protecting the group and ensuring its safety.

Within the herd, zebras engage in various social interactions. They engage in grooming behaviors, where they use their teeth to nibble and clean each other's coats. This not only helps with hygiene but also strengthens social bonds between zebras. Grooming also serves as a form of communication, as zebras use tactile sensations to convey messages such as trust and affiliation.

Another interesting aspect of zebra social behavior is their formation of temporary alliances, particularly during times of danger. When faced with a predator threat, zebras will often come together and form a tight-knit group, with their heads facing outward. This behavior, known as "mobbing," helps to confuse and deter predators, making it harder for them to single out an individual zebra.

Reproductive Behavior

Reproduction is a significant aspect of zebra behavior, with specific patterns and rituals observed within the species. Male zebras, known as stallions, engage in competitive behavior to establish dominance and gain access to potential mates. They will often engage in aggressive displays, such as charging, biting, and kicking, to establish their dominance over other males.

Female zebras, known as mares, have a cyclic reproductive pattern, with the ability to conceive at specific times during their estrous cycle. When a mare is in the fertile phase of her cycle, she will exhibit receptive behaviors, such as lifting her tail, urinating frequently, and displaying a characteristic mating stance. This signals her availability to the dominant stallion and initiates the mating process.

Once a pair has mated, the gestation period for zebras is approximately 12 to 13 months. Female zebras typically give birth to a single foal, which is highly developed at birth and capable of standing and running within a short period of time. The mother-foal bond is strong, and the mare invests significant time and energy in nurturing and protecting her offspring.

Migration Patterns

Zebras are known for their impressive migration patterns, where large herds travel long distances in search of food and water. Migration is often triggered by changes in environmental conditions, such as the onset of the dry season or the availability of fresh grazing areas.

During migration, zebras demonstrate remarkable navigational abilities, using various cues such as landmarks, celestial navigation, and memory of previous migration routes. They are also able to sense changes in temperature and humidity, allowing them to adapt their movements accordingly.

Migration serves several purposes for zebras. It allows them to access new food sources, avoid competition for resources, and reduce the risk of predation. Additionally, migration is an important social activity, as it provides opportunities for social interaction and bonding within the herd.

Summary

The natural habits and behaviors of zebras provide valuable insight into their psychology and social dynamics. Their foraging behavior highlights their adaptability to changing environments and their ability to selectively consume nutritious vegetation. Social behavior among zebras emphasizes the importance of social bonds and cooperation within the herd. Reproductive behavior highlights the complex mating rituals and the strong maternal care exhibited by female zebras. Finally, migration patterns demonstrate their remarkable navigation skills and the social benefits of group movement.

Understanding these natural habits and behaviors of zebras is essential for comprehending their psychological factors and how they interact with their environment. It allows for a deeper exploration of their cognitive processes, emotions, and developmental stages. By studying zebras in their natural habitat, we can uncover the interconnectedness between their behavior and psychology, shedding light on the complex nature of these magnificent animals.

Further Reading

If you are interested in exploring further about the natural habits and behaviors of zebras, the following resources provide in-depth information:

- Estes, R. D. (1992). The behavior guide to African mammals: Including hoofed mammals, carnivores, primates. Los Angeles, CA: University of California Press.
- Caro, T. M. (1994). Cheetahs of the Serengeti Plains: Group living in an asocial species. Chicago, IL: University of Chicago Press.
- Spinage, C. A. (2012). African ecology: Benchmarks and historical perspectives. Berlin, Germany: Springer Science & Business Media.

These resources offer a comprehensive understanding of not only the natural habits and behaviors of zebras but also the broader context of African ecology and wildlife. They provide valuable insights into the intricate relationship between animals and their environment, serving as a foundation for a deeper exploration of psychological factors in animals like zebras.

Grazing Patterns and Social Behavior

In this section, we will explore the grazing patterns and social behavior of zebras. Grazing is a fundamental behavior for zebras as it directly influences their survival, reproduction, and social interactions. By understanding the grazing patterns and social behavior of zebras, we can gain insights into their ecological role and social dynamics within their herds.

Grazing Patterns

Grazing patterns refer to the specific ways in which zebras acquire and consume food in their natural habitat. Zebras are herbivores and primarily feed on grasses, although they may also consume leaves, stems, and bark from certain trees and shrubs. The grazing patterns of zebras are influenced by several factors, including the availability and quality of food, competition for resources, and predation risk.

One important grazing pattern observed in zebras is known as patch grazing. Zebras show a preference for grazing on patches of grass rather than continuously moving and grazing across open areas. This behavior is thought to optimize resource acquisition by allowing zebras to focus on areas with higher forage quality and abundance. Patch grazing also has ecological benefits, as it promotes a diverse vegetation structure and enhances ecological heterogeneity.

Another important grazing pattern in zebras is selective grazing. Zebras display a selective feeding behavior by choosing certain plant species over others. This selectivity is influenced by factors such as nutritional content, digestibility, and palatability of plants. Zebras have evolved the ability to detect and consume plants with high nutritional value, ensuring their dietary requirements are met. This selective feeding behavior also reduces competition for limited resources within their habitat.

Social Behavior

Zebras are highly social animals and form stable social groups known as herds. Social behavior in zebras plays a crucial role in various aspects of their lives, including communication, resource sharing, predator defense, and reproduction.

One important aspect of social behavior in zebras is herd structure. Zebras typically form large herds consisting of several individuals, although smaller herds of related individuals can also occur. Within the herd, there is a hierarchical social structure based on dominance. Dominance hierarchies are established through various social interactions, including aggressive behavior and ritualized displays. The dominant individuals have priority access to resources such as food and water and often play a critical role in herd cohesion and coordination.

Zebras also exhibit affiliative behaviors, which include mutual grooming, social bonding, and play. Mutual grooming serves not only as a hygienic activity but also as a social bonding mechanism. Grooming helps to strengthen social bonds within the herd and reduce social tension. Play behavior, especially observed among young zebras, serves as a form of socialization and skill development.

In terms of reproduction, social behavior plays a vital role in mate selection and courtship. Male zebras engage in elaborate courtship displays, such as braying and neck wrestling, to attract females and establish dominance. Female zebras have the choice of selecting their mates based on these displays and other factors such as social status and genetic quality.

Case Study: Impact of Grazing Patterns and Social Behavior on Ecosystems

The grazing patterns and social behavior of zebras have significant implications for the ecosystems they inhabit. One notable example is the interaction between zebras and grasslands. Zebras' patch grazing behavior contributes to maintaining a mosaic of vegetation patches, which enhances plant diversity and creates habitats for a variety of other organisms. By selectively grazing on certain plant species, zebras play a role in shaping the composition and structure of grasslands, influencing the abundance of different plant species and their associated wildlife.

Furthermore, zebras' social behavior, particularly their herd structure and hierarchical dominance, can have cascading effects on the ecosystem. The presence of dominant individuals in the herd ensures efficient resource utilization and predator defense, benefiting the overall health and survival of the group. The cooperation and coordination within the herd also contribute to collective vigilance against predators, maximization of foraging opportunities, and overall herd success.

Understanding the ecological and behavioral interactions of zebras is crucial for the conservation and management of their populations and the ecosystems they inhabit. By recognizing the importance of grazing patterns and social behavior in zebras, we can develop effective strategies for the protection of their habitats and the preservation of their ecological role.

Key Takeaways

- Zebras exhibit patch grazing and selective feeding behaviors to optimize resource acquisition. - Social behavior in zebras involves a hierarchical structure, mutual grooming, play, and elaborate courtship displays. - Grazing patterns and social behavior of zebras have significant implications for ecosystem dynamics and biodiversity. - Understanding the ecological and behavioral interactions of zebras is important for conservation and management efforts.

Exercises

1. Explain the ecological significance of zebras' patch grazing behavior and its impact on the grasslands they inhabit.
2. Describe the process of establishing dominance hierarchies within zebra herds and the benefits of such social structures.
3. Discuss the role of mutual grooming in strengthening social bonds within zebra herds and reducing social tension.
4. Explore the importance of zebra courtship displays in mate selection and reproductive success.
5. Investigate how the social behavior of zebras contributes to their collective vigilance against predators.

Further Reading

1. Estes, R. D. (1991). The behavior guide to African mammals: Including hoofed mammals, carnivores, primates. University of California Press.
2. Rubenstein, D. I., & Hack, M. A. (2004). Natural and sexual selection and the evolution of multi-level societies: Insights from zebras with comparisons to primates. In Genetic and Cultural Evolution of Cooperation (pp. 233-247). Springer.
3. Kingdon, J. (1989). East African Mammals: An atlas of evolution in Africa. University of Chicago Press.

Predation and defense mechanisms

In the natural world, predators and their prey have engaged in an evolutionary arms race, each adapting to gain an advantage over the other. Predation plays a crucial role in shaping the behavior and psychology of zebras. In this section, we will explore the various predation strategies used by predators targeting zebras and the defense mechanisms employed by zebras to evade predation.

Predation Strategies

Predators targeting zebras employ a variety of strategies to capture their prey. These strategies are shaped by factors such as the predator's physical characteristics, hunting tactics, and the ecology of their environment. Some common predation strategies used against zebras include:

1. **Sneak Attacks:** Certain predators, like lions and cheetahs, utilize stealthy tactics to ambush their prey. They rely on their speed and ability to blend in with their surroundings to get close to the zebras unnoticed. Once in range, a sudden burst of speed is used to launch a surprise attack.

2. **Coordinated Hunting:** Predators like African wild dogs and hyenas are known for their highly organized and cooperative hunting strategies. These predators work together as a pack to surround and exhaust the zebras, eventually overwhelming them by sheer numbers and coordination.

3. **Stalking:** Some predators, such as leopards and African lions, employ stalking as a means of approaching zebras undetected. They patiently observe their prey from a distance, utilizing cover and camouflage to get closer without triggering the zebras' alarm.

4. **Selective Predation:** Certain predators selectively target weaker or vulnerable individuals among the zebra population. This strategy is commonly observed in cases where predators seek out young or injured zebras, as they are easier to capture and subdue.

Defense Mechanisms

Zebras have evolved a range of defense mechanisms to increase their chances of survival in the face of predation. These defense mechanisms can be categorized into two main types: passive defenses and active defenses.

Passive defenses involve adaptations that make zebras less attractive or visible to predators. These defenses include:

- **Camouflage:** The black and white striped coat of zebras serves as a form of camouflage, making it difficult for predators to single out a specific individual within a moving zebra herd. The disruptive coloration created by their stripes confuses predators and disrupts their ability to gauge distance and direction accurately.

- **Grouping Behavior:** Zebras often form large herds, and staying in a group provides them with protection through the "confusion effect." The overlapping stripes of multiple zebras create visual confusion for predators, making it challenging to single out a particular target.

Active defenses involve direct actions taken by zebras to deter or fend off predators. These defenses include:

- **Vigilance:** Zebras have developed heightened vigilance as a defense mechanism. They are constantly scanning their surroundings, using their acute eyesight, and the ability to rotate their ears to detect any signs of potential danger. Zebras will emit alarm calls to alert the herd of an approaching predator.

- **Aggressive Behavior:** When confronted with a predator, zebras may exhibit aggressive behaviors as a means of defense. This includes vocalizing loudly, kicking, biting, and charging at the predator. By displaying strength and aggression, zebras aim to intimidate the predator and deter it from attacking.

- **Speed and Agility:** Zebras are incredible runners, capable of reaching speeds of up to 40 miles per hour. Their ability to change direction swiftly and make sudden turns makes it challenging for predators to maintain pursuit. Zebras will often engage in evasive maneuvers to outmaneuver predators and escape potential capture.

It is important to note that while these defense mechanisms increase the chances of survival for zebras, they are not foolproof. Predation is a constant threat, and predator-prey dynamics continue to shape the behavior and psychology of zebras.

Example: The Lion and Zebra Chase

To illustrate the interplay between predator and prey, let us consider the classic example of a lion chasing a zebra. The lion, utilizing its superior strength and predatory instincts, launches a sneak attack on a zebra grazing peacefully in the open grasslands.

As the lion begins its pursuit, the zebra's natural defense mechanisms come into play. The zebra immediately detects the predator due to its acute senses of vision and hearing. It emits an alarm call, causing nearby zebras to become alert and aware of the imminent danger.

The lion, unable to rely solely on stealth during the chase due to the alarm raised by the zebra, adjusts its strategy. It starts to gain ground on the zebra, relying on its superior speed to close the distance between them. However, the zebra, with its agility and ability to change direction rapidly, makes sudden turns, evading the lion's pursuit.

The chase continues, with the lion relentlessly pursuing the zebra, and the zebra utilizing its speed and evasive maneuvers to avoid capture. Ultimately, the outcome of the chase can vary, with the zebra's defense mechanisms determining whether it successfully escapes or falls prey to the lion's hunting skills.

Caveat: Incomplete Protection

While defense mechanisms increase the zebra's chances of survival, they are not infallible. Predators, through their own evolutionary adaptations and strategies, can exploit weaknesses and vulnerabilities in the defenses employed by zebras. Natural selection constantly pushes both predator and prey to adapt and counteradapt in an ongoing struggle for survival.

Furthermore, not all predation attempts are successful. Zebras can escape from a predator's clutches, and successful defense mechanisms can thwart predation altogether. Studying the interaction between predators and zebras provides valuable insights into the complex dynamics of the natural world and the interplay between behavior and survival.

Further Reading

To delve deeper into the fascinating field of predation and defense mechanisms, the following resources are highly recommended:

- Caro, T. (2005). *Antipredator Defenses in Birds and Mammals.* Chicago, IL: University of Chicago Press.
- Estes, R. D. (1991). *The Behavior Guide to African Mammals.* Berkeley, CA: University of California Press.
- Spinage, C. A. (1994). *The Natural History of Zebras.* London, UK: T. & A.D. Poyser.
- Tinbergen, N. (1960). *The Study of Instinct.* New York, NY: Oxford University Press.

Taking a multidisciplinary approach that combines ethology, ecology, and evolutionary biology, these resources provide comprehensive insights into the remarkable adaptations and strategies employed by predators and prey in the wild.

Exercises

1. Discuss and compare the predation strategies employed by lions and cheetahs. How do their hunting tactics differ, and how do zebras respond to their respective approaches?

2. Conduct research on zebras' visual perception and their ability to detect predators. How do zebras' eyesight and color vision contribute to their defense mechanisms?

3. Imagine you are a wildlife conservationist tasked with designing a safe zone for zebras in an area with high predator activity. What measures would you implement to minimize predation risk for the zebras? Consider both passive and active defense strategies.

These exercises will enhance your understanding of the complex predator-prey dynamics and the significant role that defense mechanisms play in ensuring the survival of zebras in the face of predation.

Migration patterns and territoriality

Migration patterns and territoriality are important aspects of zebra behavior that are influenced by various psychological factors. Understanding these factors can provide valuable insights into the social dynamics and survival strategies of zebras.

Migration patterns

Zebras are known for their impressive long-distance migrations, which involve the seasonal movement of individuals or groups from one area to another. Migration serves multiple purposes for zebras, including access to food and water, avoidance of predators, and mating opportunities.

Environmental cues: Zebras rely on environmental cues, such as changes in vegetation and weather patterns, to initiate and guide their migrations. These cues signal the availability of resources and help zebras determine the timing and direction of their movements.

Group dynamics: Zebras usually migrate in large herds, which provide several benefits. Firstly, traveling in groups offers a better defense against predators, as the combined vigilance of many individuals increases the chances of detecting and evading potential threats. Secondly, being part of a herd enhances social cohesion and reduces the risk of getting separated from the group during migration.

Navigational abilities: Zebras possess remarkable navigational abilities that enable them to navigate over long distances without getting lost. They are believed to rely on a combination of visual landmarks, olfactory cues, and internal compass mechanisms to orient themselves during migration.

Leadership and coordination: During migration, zebras exhibit coordinated movement patterns, with individuals taking turns to lead the herd. This leadership rotation helps to distribute the energy expenditure among group members and ensures that no single individual bears the burden of leading for an extended period.

Seasonal variations: Migration patterns of zebras may vary depending on seasonal changes in resource availability. For example, zebras may move to areas with greener pastures during the rainy season and return to drier regions during the dry season.

Territoriality

Territoriality is another important aspect of zebra behavior, particularly in relation to defending resources and establishing social hierarchies within a population.

Resource defense: Zebras display territorial behavior to defend valuable resources such as grazing areas and water sources. By marking their territories through scent marking (urination) and rubbing against objects, zebras communicate their ownership and deter intruders from encroaching upon their resources.

Social hierarchies: Within a zebra herd, a social hierarchy exists, with dominant individuals having priority access to resources. Dominance is established through various display behaviors, including aggressive encounters such as biting and kicking. The hierarchical structure helps to minimize competition within the group and maintain order during feeding and other activities.

Territorial boundaries: Zebra territories are not strictly demarcated by physical boundaries but are maintained through social interactions and dominance displays. These boundaries are fluid and may shift over time, particularly during periods of resource scarcity or when new individuals join or leave the group.

Conflict resolution: Conflicts over resources or dominance within the herd are resolved through a series of ritualistic behaviors, such as threatening displays, vocalizations, and physical interactions. These behaviors serve to establish clear communication and avoid serious physical harm.

Mate selection: Territoriality also plays a role in mate selection among zebras. Dominant males usually have greater access to females and are more likely to successfully mate and reproduce. This hierarchical mating system helps maintain genetic diversity within the population.

Migration and territoriality: an interplay

Migration patterns and territoriality are interconnected aspects of zebra behavior. The availability of resources along migration routes influences the establishment of temporary territories during migration. These territories serve as stopover points where zebras can rest and replenish their energy reserves before continuing their journey.

Additionally, territorial behavior can affect migration patterns when zebras attempt to defend territories along their migration routes. This can result in conflicts and competition for limited resources between individuals or neighboring herds.

Understanding the interplay between migration patterns and territoriality is crucial for conservation efforts and managing zebra populations. By considering the psychological factors influencing these behaviors, such as resource availability and social dynamics, conservationists and wildlife managers can develop strategies to ensure the viability and sustainability of zebra populations.

Case study: The Great Wildebeest Migration

A prominent example of migration patterns and territoriality is the Great Wildebeest Migration in East Africa, in which zebras play a significant role. This annual migration involves millions of wildebeests, zebras, and other herbivores traveling between the Serengeti National Park in Tanzania and the Maasai Mara Reserve in Kenya.

During this migration, zebras form mixed herds with wildebeests, benefiting from the wildebeests' superior olfactory abilities to detect predators. These mixed herds exhibit complex social dynamics and have been found to have a positive effect on the survival rates of both species.

The migration route is also marked by temporary territories that zebras establish along the way. These territories provide essential grazing opportunities and access to water sources, ensuring the successful completion of the migration.

The Great Wildebeest Migration highlights the intricate relationship between migration patterns and territoriality in zebras and underscores the importance of conserving migration corridors and preserving suitable habitats for these remarkable animals.

Summary

Migration patterns and territoriality are essential aspects of zebra behavior, driven by various psychological factors. Zebras exhibit impressive long-distance migrations guided by environmental cues, group dynamics, navigational abilities, and coordinated leadership. Territoriality is manifested in resource defense, the establishment of social hierarchies, and the resolution of conflicts through ritualistic behaviors. The interplay between migration patterns and territoriality influences zebra behavior and has implications for their conservation and management. The case study of the Great Wildebeest Migration illustrates the complexity and significance of these behaviors in zebras.

Social Psychology of Zebras

Social Interaction and Communication

In this section, we will explore the fascinating world of social interaction and communication among zebras. Zebras, like many other animal species, rely on effective communication to establish and maintain social relationships within their herds. Social interaction plays a crucial role in their survival, as it facilitates cooperation, coordination, and the sharing of vital information.

Importance of Social Interaction

Social interaction among zebras serves several important functions. Firstly, it helps in the formation and maintenance of social bonds within the herd. Zebras are highly social animals and form strong social relationships with other members of their group. These bonds provide them with a sense of security and protection against potential threats.

Secondly, social interaction enables zebras to establish a social hierarchy within the herd. Like many animal species, zebras have a structured social system where certain individuals hold dominant positions, while others occupy subordinate roles. Social interaction, such as displays of aggression or submission, helps in establishing and maintaining this hierarchical order.

Thirdly, social interaction plays a crucial role in reproductive success. Zebras engage in courtship behaviors and mate selection processes, which require effective communication between individuals. Through various visual and auditory signals, zebras convey their reproductive readiness and attract potential mates.

Communication Modes

Zebras employ a variety of communication modes to interact and convey important information within their social group. These modes include visual, auditory, and olfactory signals.

Visual signals are an essential component of zebra communication. The distinct black and white stripes on their bodies serve as visual cues for individual recognition within the herd. Zebras can also communicate their intentions and emotions through body postures and facial expressions. For example, an erect mane and a stiff body posture may signal aggression, while a relaxed posture and a lowered head indicate submission.

Auditory signals play a crucial role in zebra communication, especially over long distances. Zebras produce a range of vocalizations, including whinnies, snorts, and barks, each having a specific meaning. Whinnies are used for long-distance communication, signaling the presence of potential threats or attracting other herd members.

Olfactory signals, although less prominent than visual and auditory signals, also contribute to zebra communication. They use scent marking, where zebras release pheromones through urine or glandular secretions, to convey information about their individual identity, reproductive status, and territory boundaries.

Towards an Integrated Understanding

To fully comprehend the intricacies of zebra social interaction and communication, an interdisciplinary approach combining behavioral ecology, evolutionary biology, and cognitive psychology is essential. This approach allows us to explore how social dynamics and communication strategies have evolved in zebras and how they impact their survival and reproductive success.

By studying social interaction and communication among zebras, researchers can gain insights into the complex mechanisms underlying animal societies. This knowledge has practical applications, ranging from conservation strategies to animal welfare practices. Moreover, understanding zebra communication can provide inspiration for human communication and collaboration, as some principles of effective communication are shared across species.

Overall, social interaction and communication form the bedrock of zebra society. Through visual, auditory, and olfactory signals, zebras establish social bonds, maintain hierarchical structures, and ensure successful reproduction. Their communication strategies provide us with valuable insights into the fundamental nature of social interaction and the importance of effective communication in humans and other animal species.

Example Problem:

A researcher is interested in studying the different visual signals exhibited by zebras during social interaction. They hypothesize that specific body postures and facial expressions convey distinct meanings.

Solution:

To test the hypothesis, the researcher observes a group of zebras in their natural habitat and records the various body postures and facial expressions displayed during social interactions. They also note the context in which each behavior occurs. The data collected can then be analyzed using descriptive statistics to identify patterns and associations between behaviors and their meanings. The researcher can further validate their findings by conducting experiments or comparing their observations with existing literature on zebra behavior and communication.

This study not only contributes to our understanding of zebra communication but also provides insights into the universality of certain visual communication signals across species.

The Psychological Factors in Zebras

Studying herds and social hierarchy

Studying the herds and social hierarchy of zebras is vital for understanding their social behavior and dynamics. Zebras are highly social animals that live in stable social groups known as herds. In this section, we will explore the methods used to study these herds and the concept of social hierarchy among zebras.

Importance of studying herds

Herding is a fundamental aspect of zebra behavior, as they rely on the collective strength and cooperation of the group for various survival advantages. By studying herds, researchers can gain insights into the social dynamics, communication systems, and decision-making processes of zebras.

Herds provide zebras with protection from predators, as larger groups increase their chances of detecting and deterring potential threats. Additionally, herding allows zebras to access resources such as food and water more efficiently, reducing competition and ensuring survival.

Understanding how herds function and how zebras interact within them is crucial for comprehending the intricate social behaviors exhibited by these animals. It helps us uncover the complex web of relationships, dominance structures, and social roles that shape zebra society.

Methods of studying herds

To study herds and social hierarchy in zebras, researchers employ a combination of observational and experimental methods. Here are some common approaches used:

1. **Ethological observations:** Ethologists observe zebras in their natural habitat to study their herding behavior. They collect data on group size, composition, movement patterns, and interactions between individuals. This type of observation provides insights into the daily routines, feeding habits, and social interactions of zebras within a herd.

2. **Social network analysis:** Social network analysis is a valuable tool for understanding the dynamics of social relationships within zebra herds. By observing and mapping the interactions between individuals, researchers can identify patterns of association, determine the strength of relationships, and analyze the flow of information within the group. This approach helps unravel the social hierarchy and the role of specific individuals within the herd.

3. **Dominance hierarchies:** Dominance hierarchies play a crucial role in zebra herds, as they establish social order and reduce conflict. Researchers study dominance interactions, such as aggressive encounters, displacements, and submission behaviors, to determine the rank and status of individual zebras within the hierarchy. This information sheds light on power dynamics, access to resources, and reproductive success.

4. **Experimental manipulations:** Researchers also conduct controlled experiments to investigate the effects of certain factors on herd behavior and social hierarchy. For example, they may alter group composition, resource distribution, or the presence of predators to observe how these factors influence zebra interactions. These experiments help test hypotheses and provide valuable insights into the decision-making processes and adaptability of zebras in different situations.

Social hierarchy in zebras

Zebras exhibit a social hierarchy within their herds, characterized by dominance relationships among group members. The social hierarchy determines access to resources, mating opportunities, and social interactions. Here are some key aspects of social hierarchy in zebras:

- **Dominance ranks:** Zebras establish dominance ranks based on aggression and submission behaviors. Higher-ranking individuals have priority access to resources, such as food and water, and are more successful in reproduction. Dominance ranks are often stable, but they can change through aggressive encounters and displacements.

- **Territoriality:** Within the herd, individual zebras establish personal spaces known as territories. These territories provide a sense of security and control over resources. Dominant individuals usually have larger territories and defend them from lower-ranking individuals.

- **Benefits of social hierarchy:** Social hierarchy in zebras is advantageous for several reasons. It helps reduce aggression and conflict within the herd by establishing clear dominance relationships. It ensures efficient resource access and optimizes reproduction, as higher-ranking individuals have better chances of mating and securing resources for their offspring.

- **Stability and flexibility:** While dominance ranks are generally stable, they can change in response to individual abilities, age, and environmental factors. Younger zebras may challenge higher-ranking individuals, leading to rank changes. The flexibility of the social hierarchy allows for adaptation and ensures the survival and success of the herd as a whole.

Example: Social hierarchy in a zebra herd

To illustrate the concept of social hierarchy, let's consider a zebra herd consisting of 15 individuals. Through observational studies and social network analysis, researchers have identified the following dominance relationships and interactions:

- Zebra A is the highest-ranking individual and displays dominant behaviors towards others. It has priority access to resources such as grazing areas and water sources.

- Zebras B, C, and D have intermediate ranks and show submission behaviors towards Zebra A. They have access to resources but are subordinate to Zebra A.

- Zebras E to O occupy the lower ranks, with individual dominance relationships among them. They have limited access to resources and often face aggression from higher-ranking individuals.

The social hierarchy ensures that each zebra knows its place within the herd and helps maintain order and harmony. Lower-ranking zebras may form alliances or seek opportunities to challenge higher-ranking individuals to improve their status.

Further research and areas of study

While much research has been conducted on herds and social hierarchy in zebras, there are still several avenues for further exploration. Some potential areas of study include:

- Investigating the impact of environmental factors, such as habitat quality and availability of resources, on the stability and dynamics of zebra herds.

- Examining the role of social bonds and affiliative behaviors in the formation and maintenance of social hierarchy within zebras, and comparing it with other social species.

- Exploring the effects of human-induced disturbances, such as habitat fragmentation and tourism, on zebra herds and social hierarchy.

- Using innovative technological tools, such as GPS tracking and bioacoustic analysis, to gather more precise data on zebra movements, communication, and interactions within herds.

Understanding the intricate social dynamics of zebra herds and the concept of social hierarchy paves the way for a deeper comprehension of animal behavior, social cognition, and the application of this knowledge in various fields, including conservation, ethology, and animal welfare. By studying herds and social hierarchy, we gain insights into the fascinating world of zebra society and the factors that shape their behaviors and interactions.

Non-verbal communication among Zebras

Non-verbal communication plays a vital role in the social dynamics of zebras. While they may not communicate using spoken language, zebras rely on a complex system of visual signals, postures, and movements to convey messages to one another. Understanding these non-verbal cues is essential to comprehend the social structure and interactions within zebra herds.

Visual signals and postures

Zebras employ various visual signals and postures to communicate their intentions, emotions, and social status. One such signal is the position of their ears. When zebras hold their ears forward, it typically indicates alertness and attentiveness. On the other hand, when their ears are pinned back, it signals aggression or submission, depending on the context.

Another crucial visual cue utilized by zebras is body posture. Dominant zebras often display a tall, upright stance with their heads held high, signifying their authority and power within the group. Conversely, subordinate individuals adopt a more relaxed, low-profile posture to convey submission and respect.

Facial expressions and tail movements

Like other animals, zebras employ facial expressions and tail movements to communicate their emotions and intentions. Zebras can use their facial muscles to display a range of expressions, including raising their eyebrows, wrinkling their nostrils, and curling their lips. These expressions can convey emotions such as fear, aggression, or contentment.

Tail movements also play a crucial role in zebra communication. When zebras hold their tails straight up, it signals a state of high alertness or excitement. Conversely, a tucked or relaxed tail indicates a calm or submissive demeanor. Zebras may also vigorously swish their tails back and forth as a warning sign to potential predators or as a mechanism to ward off flies and parasites.

Body language and locomotion

Zebras utilize body language and locomotion as non-verbal communication tools to express their social status and intentions. Dominant zebras often demonstrate their authority by engaging in confident, purposeful movements with a high head and raised neck. They may also exhibit behaviors like chasing, kicking, or biting to assert their dominance over subordinate individuals.

Subordinate zebras, on the other hand, display deferential body language to avoid confrontations. They may adopt a more meandering gait, lower their heads, or even retreat to create physical distance from dominant individuals.

Integration of non-verbal cues

Zebras integrate multiple non-verbal cues in their communication, creating a nuanced and intricate system. By combining visual signals, facial expressions, tail movements, and body language, zebras can convey a rich array of messages to one another. These cues serve to establish social hierarchies, communicate warnings or threats, express submission or dominance, and facilitate coordination within the group.

Example: Communication during a zebra fight

To illustrate the importance of non-verbal communication among zebras, let's consider a scenario where two zebras engage in a fight over access to resources. In this situation, the zebra with higher social status communicates its dominance through assertive body language, such as holding its ears forward, standing tall, and displaying aggressive facial expressions.

The subordinate zebra, recognizing the dominant individual's signals, responds with submissive non-verbal cues. It may lower its head, pin back its ears, and display a relaxed tail. These non-verbal signals communicate the submissive zebra's recognition of the dominant individual's authority and its willingness to concede the disputed resource.

By relying on non-verbal communication, zebras can successfully establish and maintain a social order within their herds, minimizing conflict and facilitating cooperation.

Resources for further exploration

To delve deeper into the topic of non-verbal communication among zebras, the following resources provide valuable insights:

- Tinbergen, N. (1953). "The Herring Gull's World." A classic work that explores animal behavior, including non-verbal communication, from an ethological perspective.

- Kingdon, J. (1989). "East African Mammals: An Atlas of Evolution in Africa." This comprehensive atlas includes detailed illustrations and descriptions of various zebra species, including their behavior and communication methods.

- McComb, K., Shannon, G., Durant, S. M., Sayialel, S., Slotow, R., & Poole, J. (2011). "Leadership in elephants: the adaptive value of age." This study on elephants highlights the importance of non-verbal communication in social animals and can provide insights applicable to zebras.

Exercise

Consider a scenario in which a zebra herd encounters a potential predator. Discuss the non-verbal cues that zebras might display to warn others of danger and coordinate their defense. How might the expression of these cues differ between dominant and subordinate individuals?

Write a short paragraph describing the potential predator's reaction to the zebras' non-verbal communication and how it may impact their hunting strategy.

Vocalizations and their meanings

Vocalizations play a crucial role in the social communication among zebras. These distinctive sounds are used to convey a range of messages, from expressing individual identity to signaling danger or coordinating group movements. In this section, we will explore the various vocalizations produced by zebras and delve into their meanings.

Types of Zebra Vocalizations

Zebras utilize a repertoire of vocalizations that serve different communicative purposes in their social interactions. These vocalizations can be classified into several distinct types:

1. **The Braying Call:** This is the most recognizable vocalization of zebras and is commonly referred to as a "bray." It is a loud, prolonged call characterized by a series of braying sounds, similar to a donkey's call. Zebras produce braying calls when they feel threatened, to alert others in the group about potential danger.

2. **The Whinny Call:** The whinny call is a short, high-pitched vocalization produced by zebras. It is characterized by a series of rapid, ascending and descending notes. Zebras use whinny calls as a means of greeting or indicating friendly intentions towards other herd members.

3. **The Snorting Call:** Snorting calls are quick, forceful exhalations produced by zebras through their nostrils. These calls are often accompanied by a distinct puffing sound. Zebras primarily use snorting calls as an alarm signal in response to potential threats. The sound of snorting calls can also serve to ward off predators.

4. **The Nicker Call:** The nicker call is a soft, low-pitched vocalization produced by zebras. It is used primarily as a means of communication between mothers and their offspring. Zebras may also use nicker calls during grooming interactions or to express contentment and relaxation.

Interpreting Vocalizations

The vocalizations produced by zebras convey important information, allowing individuals to communicate with each other effectively. While the exact meanings of vocalizations may vary depending on the context, there are general patterns that can help us interpret their messages.

- **Threat and Alarm:** The braying call and snorting call are vocalizations that indicate potential danger or threat. When zebras sense the presence of a predator or perceive an imminent threat, they produce these vocalizations to alert others in the group and initiate a coordinated response, such as fleeing or forming a defensive formation.

- **Social Bonding:** The whinny call and nicker call are vocalizations associated with social bonding and communication within the herd. Whinny calls are often used during greetings or to reinforce social bonds between herd members. The nicker call, on the other hand, is primarily used by mothers to communicate with their young, strengthening the maternal bond and facilitating recognition between mother and offspring.

- **Individual Identity:** Each zebra has a unique braying call, which functions as a form of individual identification. This allows zebras to recognize and locate specific individuals within a group, even in dense vegetation or during blurred visual conditions. By using distinct vocalizations, zebras can maintain social cohesion and establish individual relationships within the herd.

The Role of Vocalizations in Zebra Behavior

Vocalizations play a crucial role in shaping the behavior of zebras. By using vocal signals, zebras can coordinate their movements, regulate social interactions, and respond effectively to potential threats. Here are a few examples of the behavioral significance of vocalizations:

- **Group Cohesion:** Vocalizations facilitate group cohesion among zebras. When zebras communicate through vocal signals, they reinforce social bonds, maintain contact with group members, and synchronize their movements. This coordination is particularly important during activities like migration, foraging, and predator avoidance.
- **Anti-Predator Defense:** The alarm calls of zebras, such as the braying call and snorting call, serve as effective anti-predator defense mechanisms. These vocalizations not only alert other members of the group but also act as a deterrent to predators. By producing loud and distinct sounds, zebras attempt to intimidate potential threats and discourage predatory attacks.
- **Social Hierarchy:** Vocalizations also play a role in establishing and maintaining social hierarchy within zebra herds. Through vocal communication, dominant individuals can assert their status and signal their position within the group, while subordinates may use vocalizations to acknowledge the dominance of others, ensuring social order and minimizing aggression.

Further Exploration

To gain a deeper understanding of vocalizations and their meanings in zebras, researchers employ a variety of approaches. Advanced audio recording and analysis techniques, coupled with behavioral observations, help identify and classify different vocalizations precisely. By studying the context in which vocalizations occur and analyzing the accompanying behaviors, researchers can make more accurate interpretations of zebra communication.

Understanding the vocalizations of zebras not only enriches our knowledge of their behavior but also provides insights into the evolutionary development of communication systems in ungulates. This, in turn, may have implications for other social animals with similar vocalization patterns.

Summary

Vocalizations are a vital component of zebra communication, serving various functions such as threat signaling, social bonding, and individual identification. Through braying calls, whinny calls, snorting calls, and nicker calls, zebras convey information that facilitates group cohesion, anti-predator defense, and establishment of social hierarchy. Further research and analysis of vocalizations will undoubtedly contribute to our understanding of these fascinating animals and their complex social lives.

Further Reading

- McComb, K., Reby, D., Baker, L., & Moss, C. (2003). African elephants show high levels of interest in the skulls and ivory of their own species. Biology Letters, 271(Suppl 6), S340-S341. https://doi.org/10.1098/rsbl.2003.0147
- Larom, D., Garstang, M., & Symonds, M. (1997). Electronic identification of the contacts between separate branches of free-ranging zebra herds. Animal Behaviour, 54(1), 155-166. https://doi.org/10.1006/anbe.1996.0434
- Nandintsetseg, D., Ueno, A., Teramoto, M., Hara, F., & Tsukamoto, M. (2018). Fission-fusion dynamics in a population of Mongolian gazelles with synchronized two-level grouping. Journal of Ethology, 36(1), 79-85. https://doi.org/10.1007/s10164-017-0525-3

Exercises

1. Observe a zebra group at a zoo or in the wild (if possible) and document their vocalizations. Try to identify the different types of vocalizations and their corresponding behavioral contexts.
2. Research other ungulate species and compare their vocalizations with those of zebras. What similarities and differences do you notice? How might these vocalizations be adaptive in their respective environments?
3. Conduct a mock study to investigate the effects of different vocalizations on zebra behavior. Design an experiment that manipulates the presence or absence of specific vocalizations and measures subsequent behavioral responses.

Caveats and Limitations

Studies on zebra vocalizations are challenging due to the complex nature of vocal communication in the wild. Factors such as environmental noise, the distance between the observer and the subject, and variations in vocalization context can make data collection and interpretation difficult. Additionally, generalizations based on limited observations should be made cautiously.

It is important to remember that zebra vocalizations are just one aspect of their overall communication system, which also includes body postures, facial expressions, and olfactory signals. To gain a comprehensive understanding of zebra behavior, researchers must consider these multiple modes of communication and their interplay.

Cognitive Processes in Zebras

Memory and Learning in Zebras

Memory and learning are essential psychological processes that play a vital role in the behavior and survival of zebras. In this section, we will explore how zebras encode, store, and retrieve information, as well as their ability to learn from their environment and adapt their behavior accordingly.

Memory Processes in Zebras

Zebras possess a remarkable capacity for memory, allowing them to remember important information about their environment and past experiences. One important aspect of their memory is spatial memory, which refers to their ability to remember and navigate through their habitat.

Zebras exhibit impressive spatial memory skills, enabling them to remember the location of food and water sources, as well as the routes to specific grazing areas and migration routes. This ability is crucial for their survival in the often challenging and expansive savannah environments they inhabit. Zebras can rely on landmarks and spatial cues to navigate their surroundings, forming mental maps that guide their movements.

Additionally, zebras demonstrate a form of associative memory, allowing them to learn and remember associations between different stimuli. For example, they can learn to associate the presence of predators, such as lions or hyenas, with certain visual or auditory cues. This learned association helps them identify potential threats and respond accordingly, either by fleeing or adopting defensive behaviors.

Learning Processes in Zebras

In addition to their remarkable memory capabilities, zebras also exhibit impressive learning abilities. Learning refers to the process of acquiring new knowledge or skills through experience or training. Zebras can learn from various sources, including their interactions with their environment, other zebras, and their own past experiences.

Zebras learn through a process called habituation, which involves the gradual reduction of a response to a repeated or unchanging stimulus. This process is crucial for zebras to adapt to their environment and distinguish between relevant and irrelevant stimuli. For example, if zebras are repeatedly exposed to harmless sounds or movements in their habitat, they will gradually become less responsive to them, allowing them to focus on more critical stimuli.

Associative learning is another essential learning process in zebras. They can form associations between specific events or stimuli, allowing them to predict outcomes based on these associations. For instance, if zebras learn that certain visual or auditory cues are consistently followed by the presence of predators, they can associate these cues with danger and respond accordingly by initiating flight or defensive behaviors.

Zebras also demonstrate problem-solving abilities, particularly when faced with challenges related to obtaining food or water. They can devise and employ various strategies to overcome obstacles and access resources. For example, zebras have been observed using their teeth and hooves to access water from partially frozen ponds or digging through snow to reach vegetation during harsh winters.

Overall, memory and learning are critical psychological processes in zebras, enabling them to navigate their environment, recognize threats, and adapt their behaviors for survival. Understanding these processes not only provides insights into zebra behavior but also offers valuable perspectives for understanding memory and learning in other animal species, including humans.

Challenges and Limitations

Studying memory and learning in zebras poses several challenges due to the inherent difficulties in observing and measuring these processes in the wild. Additionally, ethical considerations must be taken into account to ensure the well-being of the animals during research studies. Researchers often employ non-invasive techniques such as behavioral observations and cognitive tests to assess memory and learning abilities in zebras.

Another challenge lies in the interpretation and generalizability of research findings. While studies conducted on captive zebras can provide valuable insights, the behaviors exhibited in captivity may not fully reflect the complexities of natural behaviors in the wild. It is essential to consider the ecological and social context in which zebras live to better understand their memory and learning abilities.

Despite these challenges, ongoing research and advancements in non-invasive research techniques continue to enhance our understanding of memory and learning in zebras. By addressing these challenges and limitations, we can uncover further insights into the cognitive abilities of zebras and their adaptive significance in a changing environment.

Further Reading

For further reading on memory and learning in zebras, we recommend the following resources:

1. *The Memory Process: Neuroscientific and Humanistic Perspectives* by Suzanne Nalbantian, Paul M. Matthews, and James L. McClelland.

2. *Learning and Behavior: A Contemporary Synthesis* by Mark E. Bouton and Todd R. Schachtman.

3. *Animal Cognition: Evolution, Behavior, and Cognition* by Clive D.L. Wynne.

4. *Animal Minds: Beyond Cognition to Consciousness* by Donald R. Griffin.

These resources delve into the broader concepts of memory and learning, providing valuable perspectives on the topic beyond the scope of zebras specifically.

Habituation and Associative Learning

In the study of psychological factors in zebras, one important aspect to consider is the role of habituation and associative learning in their behavior and cognition. Habituation refers to the process of an organism becoming less responsive to a repeated or irrelevant stimulus over time. Associative learning, on the other hand, involves the formation of associations between stimuli, behaviors, and outcomes. Understanding these processes is crucial for comprehending how zebras adapt to their environment and acquire new skills and knowledge.

Habituation in Zebras

Habituation plays a significant role in the behaviors and responses of zebras to both internal and external stimuli. When exposed to recurring stimuli that pose no threat or significance, zebras tend to reduce their reactions and responses over time. For example, if a zebra is repeatedly exposed to a benign sound, such as the rustling of leaves, it will gradually habituate to the sound and eventually pay less attention to it. This allows zebras to allocate their attention and energy to more relevant and potentially threatening stimuli.

Habituation can also occur in response to predators. Zebras living in areas with a high concentration of predators, such as lions or hyenas, may habituate to their presence and exhibit reduced vigilance over time. This habituation enables zebras to conserve energy and focus on essential activities such as foraging and social interactions.

Associative Learning in Zebras

Associative learning in zebras involves the formation of connections between stimuli and behavioral responses. This type of learning enables zebras to adapt to their environment, acquire new skills, and modify their behaviors based on past experiences.

One form of associative learning that zebras engage in is classical conditioning. In classical conditioning, a neutral stimulus is paired with a meaningful or biologically significant stimulus, leading to a learned response. For example, zebras may associate the sound of a predator's growl (meaningful stimulus) with the visual appearance of the predator (neutral stimulus). This association allows zebras to elicit fear and initiate appropriate defensive behaviors when they encounter similar visual or auditory cues in the future.

Another type of associative learning is operant conditioning. In operant conditioning, behaviors are strengthened or weakened based on their consequences. Zebras learn through trial and error which behaviors yield positive outcomes and which lead to negative outcomes. For instance, if a zebra discovers that grazing in a certain area leads to a better food supply, it will likely continue to graze in that location. Conversely, if a zebra receives a negative consequence, such as an aggressive encounter with another zebra, it may modify its behavior to avoid similar situations in the future.

Implications and Applications

Understanding habituation and associative learning in zebras has important implications for their survival and well-being. By habituating to non-threatening stimuli and conserving energy, zebras can better allocate their resources to essential activities. Additionally, the ability to form associations between stimuli and responses allows zebras to learn from their experiences, adapt their behaviors, and increase their chances of survival.

From an applied perspective, the knowledge of habituation and associative learning can inform conservation efforts and wildlife management practices. For instance, understanding how zebras habituate to human presence can help minimize the disturbance caused by ecotourism activities. Similarly, applying principles of operant conditioning can be used to train captive zebras in zoos, facilitating their care and ensuring their welfare.

In conclusion, habituation and associative learning are important psychological factors in the behavior and cognition of zebras. Habituation enables zebras to reduce their responsiveness to irrelevant stimuli, while associative learning allows zebras to form connections between stimuli and behavioral responses. By understanding these processes, researchers and wildlife managers can gain valuable insights into how zebras adapt to their environment and develop effective strategies for their conservation and well-being.

Spatial awareness and navigation in Zebras

Spatial awareness and navigation are crucial aspects of an animal's survival and behavior. Zebras, with their intricate social systems and extensive ranges, rely on their spatial awareness and navigational abilities to locate resources, avoid predators, and maintain social bonds. In this section, we will explore the fascinating world of zebra spatial cognition, including their ability to perceive and navigate through space.

Perception of the environment

To understand how zebras navigate their environment, it is important to first examine how they perceive and interpret the physical world around them. Zebras primarily rely on their visual and auditory senses to gather information about their surroundings. Their eyes are strategically positioned on the sides of their heads, providing them with a wide field of vision. This enables them to detect potential threats or resources from multiple angles.

Zebras possess excellent depth perception, allowing them to accurately judge distances between objects in their environment. This is particularly important for navigating through varied terrains, such as grasslands and forests, where obstacles and predators may be encountered. Additionally, their keen sense of hearing enables them to detect and locate the sounds of approaching predators or the vocalizations of other herd members.

Spatial memory and cognitive mapping

Spatial memory plays a vital role in zebra navigation. Zebras have been shown to possess an impressive ability to remember and mentally map their environment. They can remember the location of watering holes, grazing areas, and safe resting spots, even when these locations are located kilometers away.

To understand how zebras develop and use spatial memory, researchers have conducted studies using maze tasks. These experiments demonstrate that zebras are capable of learning and remembering complex spatial information. By exploring their surroundings and forming cognitive maps, zebras can accurately navigate through their environment, even when faced with changes or novel situations.

Orientation and landmark-based navigation

Zebras utilize various strategies for orientation and navigation, with one prominent method being landmark-based navigation. Landmarks are distinctive features in the environment that serve as reference points, helping zebras to establish their position and navigate in a particular direction. These landmarks can be physical features such as trees or rocks or even social cues like the presence of other herd members.

Zebras have shown an ability to recognize and remember specific landmarks, using them as beacons to guide their movements. They can also use the relative positions of multiple landmarks to determine their location and navigate towards desirable locations. This landmark-based navigation system allows zebras to efficiently move across their vast ranges while maintaining awareness of their surroundings.

Magnetic orientation

Recent studies suggest that zebras may also possess the ability to sense the Earth's magnetic field and use it for orientation. This phenomenon, known as magnetic orientation, has been observed in some bird species and sea turtles. Although the mechanisms behind magnetic orientation in zebras are not yet fully understood, it has been proposed that they may rely on specialized magnetoreceptive cells in their bodies.

The exact role of magnetic orientation in zebra navigation remains a topic of ongoing research. However, it is thought that this ability, combined with their visual and auditory perception, provides zebras with a multi-modal navigation system that enhances their spatial awareness and helps them maintain their orientation during long-distance movements and migrations.

Challenges and future directions

While much progress has been made in understanding the spatial awareness and navigation abilities of zebras, there are still many unanswered questions and challenges. One of the primary challenges is studying these behaviors in the wild, where zebras face a multitude of environmental factors that can influence their navigation strategies.

Future research could focus on using advanced tracking technologies to gather more detailed data on zebra movements and behaviors in natural habitats. Additionally, further investigation into the mechanisms behind magnetic orientation in zebras could provide valuable insights into their navigational abilities and potentially yield applications in other fields, such as robotics or biomimicry.

Understanding the spatial awareness and navigation of zebras not only enhances our knowledge of these magnificent animals but also offers valuable lessons for human navigation and design principles. By unraveling the complexities of zebra cognition, we can gain insights into our own cognitive processes and potentially apply this knowledge to improve human spatial awareness and navigation systems.

Exercises

1. Imagine you are a zebra researcher tasked with studying the spatial awareness and navigation abilities of zebras in a specific ecosystem. Design a research study outlining the methods you would use to collect data and analyze the results.

2. Conduct a field observation or virtual simulation of a zebra herd in their natural habitat. Document their spatial behaviors, such as grazing patterns, movement in relation to landmarks, and interactions with other herd members.

3. Research and discuss a specific zebra migration route. Describe the notable landmarks, environmental factors, and potential challenges zebras encounter during their journey.

Further Reading

- Kingdon, J. (1982). East African Mammals: An Atlas of Evolution in Africa (Vol. 3, Part 1). University Of Chicago Press.

- Wyman, M. T., & Wascher, C. A. F. (2020). The Magnetic Compass Mechanism of Birds and Its Role in Navigation. Journal of Experimental Biology, 223(Pt Suppl 1), jeb220574.

- Poliaková, M., Radford, A. N., & Hemelrijk, C. K. (2018). Using Virtual Reality to Study Animal Behavior and its underlying mechanisms—Case Studies in Fish, Birds and Primates. Frontiers in Psychology, 9, 2252.

In this section, we delved into the spatial awareness and navigation abilities of zebras. We explored their perception of the environment, including visual and auditory senses. We discussed the importance of spatial memory and cognitive mapping in their navigation process. Additionally, we touched on landmark-based navigation and the potential role of magnetic orientation. To truly appreciate the complexity of zebra spatial cognition, it is essential to address the challenges in studying these behaviors and explore future research directions. Through a deeper understanding of zebra navigation, we can gain valuable insights that may have implications for human navigation systems and design principles.

Problem-solving abilities of Zebras

In this section, we will explore the problem-solving abilities of zebras. Problem-solving is a cognitive process that involves the application of knowledge and skills to find solutions to unfamiliar or complex situations. Just like humans and many other animals, zebras possess problem-solving abilities that enable them to adapt to their environment and overcome challenges.

Introduction to Problem-solving

Problem-solving is a fundamental cognitive process that encompasses various steps, including problem identification, goal setting, generating alternative solutions, evaluating options, making decisions, and implementing the chosen solution. It requires cognitive flexibility, critical thinking, and the ability to effectively use memory and learning.

Zebras and Problem-solving

Zebras exhibit remarkable problem-solving abilities, which are essential for their survival in their natural habitats. Let's explore some examples of problem-solving scenarios in zebras.

Locating Water Sources Zebras inhabit grassland areas where water sources may be scarce or spread out. When faced with the problem of finding water, zebras use their sensory perception and memory to locate potential water sources. They can remember the locations of watering holes, even when they are temporarily dry, and navigate long distances to access water. This ability to solve the problem of finding water is crucial for their survival.

Escaping Predators Predation is a constant threat for zebras in the wild. When faced with the problem of escaping from predators, zebras employ various strategies. They rely on their speed and agility to outrun predators, but they also exhibit sophisticated decision-making abilities. For example, when a zebra senses danger, it assesses the situation, evaluates different escape routes, and chooses the most advantageous path to avoid being caught.

Navigating Complex Terrain Zebras often encounter challenging terrains, such as dense vegetation or rocky landscapes. In these situations, zebras demonstrate problem-solving skills by carefully assessing the environment, considering different paths, and making decisions to navigate the obstacles. They utilize their spatial awareness, memory, and sensory perception to find the most efficient route, ensuring their safety and survival.

Cognitive Processes Involved in Problem-solving

Various cognitive processes contribute to the problem-solving abilities of zebras. Let's explore some of the key cognitive processes involved:

Memory and Learning Memory plays a crucial role in problem-solving. Zebras have excellent spatial memory, allowing them to remember the locations of water sources, safe areas, and escape routes. They can also learn from past experiences, making adjustments and improving their problem-solving strategies over time.

Trial-and-error Learning Zebras engage in trial-and-error learning when faced with new challenges. They experiment with different approaches to solve problems and learn from their successes and failures. For example, when faced with a barrier, zebras may attempt different ways to overcome it, such as jumping or finding an alternative path. Through trial and error, they acquire new problem-solving skills.

Social Learning Zebras are social animals, and they can also learn problem-solving skills from observing and imitating other zebras. They learn from the experiences and strategies of their herd mates, which accelerates the acquisition of problem-solving abilities. Social learning is particularly important in situations where individual zebras encounter new or challenging problems.

Example: Crossing a River

To illustrate the problem-solving abilities of zebras, let's examine the challenge of crossing a river. Zebras often face this problem during migrations or when they encounter water bodies in their territories. When a zebra encounters a river, it must find a safe and efficient way to cross it.

Zebras exhibit an impressive level of problem-solving in these situations. First, they use their sensory perception and visual cues to assess the depth and speed of the river. They will observe other zebras or animals crossing the river and learn from their behavior. The decision-making process involves a balance between risk-taking and minimizing potential danger.

Once the zebras have gathered enough information, they may form a group and engage in cooperative problem-solving. This collaboration allows them to manage the risks associated with crossing the river. The zebras create a hierarchy, with the dominant individuals leading the way, followed by others. This strategic planning ensures the safety of the group and reduces the chances of individual zebras facing difficulties.

During the crossing, zebras may encounter unforeseen challenges, such as strong currents or steep riverbanks. In such cases, they exhibit adaptability by adjusting their crossing strategy. For example, they may change the crossing point or alter the formation to provide better support. This flexibility and problem-solving mindset enable zebras to successfully navigate and overcome the difficulties associated with crossing a river.

Tricks and Tips

Here are some tips for understanding and enhancing the problem-solving abilities of zebras:

- Encourage exploration: Providing zebras with opportunities to explore their environment promotes cognitive development and problem-solving skills. Enrichment activities such as puzzle feeders or novel objects can engage their curiosity and stimulate problem-solving behaviors.

- Foster social interaction: Zebras are social animals, and social interaction plays a significant role in their problem-solving abilities. Encouraging socialization within a herd setting can enhance their cooperative problem-solving skills.

- Create problem-solving challenges: Introducing problem-solving challenges specific to zebras can help develop their cognitive abilities. For example, placing obstacles in their habitat that require them to find a way around or solve simple puzzles can stimulate their problem-solving instincts.

Conclusion

The problem-solving abilities of zebras are a testament to their cognitive adaptability. From finding water sources to escaping predators, zebras exhibit a range of problem-solving strategies. Through the engagement of cognitive processes such as memory, learning, trial-and-error, and social learning, zebras adapt to their ever-changing environment. Understanding the problem-solving abilities of zebras not only provides insights into their behavior but also offers valuable lessons for problem-solving in human contexts.

Exercises

1. Imagine you are a zebra in the wild facing the problem of escaping from a predator. Describe the steps you would take to evaluate your options and decide on the best course of action.

2. Research and discuss a specific example of cooperative problem-solving observed in zebras. What challenges did the zebras face, and how did they collaborate to overcome them?

3. Design an enrichment activity for zebras that encourages problem-solving behavior. Consider their natural behaviors and cognitive abilities to create a stimulating and engaging challenge.

Resources

- Beran, M. J. (2015). Evolutionary perspectives on solving novel problems by nonhuman animals. Learning and Behavior, 43(4), 311-320.

- Waring, G. H., & Cleland, E. E. (2020). Foraging ecology influences memory and decision-making in a large herbivore. Ecology and Evolution, 10(17), 8890-8900.

- Reader, S. M., & Laland, K. N. (2002). Social intelligence, innovation, and enhanced brain size in primates. Proceedings of the National Academy of Sciences, 99(7), 4436-4441.

Conclusion

In conclusion, zebras possess impressive problem-solving abilities that enable them to adapt and thrive in their environments. By utilizing cognitive processes such as memory, trial-and-error learning, and social learning, zebras can overcome challenges like finding water sources, escaping from predators, and navigating complex terrains. Understanding the problem-solving abilities of zebras provides valuable insights into their behavior and sheds light on the cognitive capabilities of animals. The study of zebras' problem-solving abilities also has implications for problem-solving research in the broader field of animal cognition.

Emotions and Motivation in Zebras

Examining Fear and Anxiety in Zebras

Fear and anxiety are fundamental emotions that play a crucial role in the lives of both humans and animals. In this section, we will explore the concept of fear and anxiety in zebras, examining their behavioral responses, underlying mechanisms, and the adaptive advantages that these emotions confer.

Behavioral Responses to Fear and Anxiety

When faced with a perceived threat, zebras exhibit a range of behavioral responses that reflect their fear and anxiety. One of the most common responses is freezing, where zebras momentarily stop moving to assess the situation. This freezing behavior allows zebras to blend in with their surroundings and avoid detection by potential predators.

In addition to freezing, zebras may also engage in fleeing or running behaviors to escape from the threat. This rapid movement helps them to increase the distance between themselves and the perceived danger. Zebras often display zigzag running patterns, which make it difficult for predators to predict their trajectory and catch them.

Another typical response to fear and anxiety in zebras is vigilance. Zebras become more alert and actively scan their surroundings for potential threats. This heightened vigilance allows them to detect predators early and take appropriate action to ensure their safety.

Underlying Mechanisms of Fear and Anxiety

The experience of fear and anxiety in zebras is associated with a complex interplay of physiological and cognitive processes. When faced with a threat, the amygdala, a region in the zebra's brain responsible for processing emotions, becomes activated. This activation triggers a cascade of physiological responses that prepare the zebra for a fight-or-flight response.

The release of stress hormones, such as adrenaline and cortisol, prepares the zebra's body for immediate action. These hormones increase heart rate, blood pressure, and respiratory rate, providing the necessary energy for the zebra to respond to the threat effectively.

Cognitively, fear and anxiety in zebras are influenced by past experiences and learned associations. Zebras can learn to associate certain cues or situations with danger, leading to the development of conditioned fear responses. For example, if a zebra encounters a predator in a specific area, it may become anxious when revisiting that location in the future.

Adaptive Advantages of Fear and Anxiety

Fear and anxiety have adaptive advantages for zebras, enabling them to survive in their natural environment. These emotions help zebras to detect and respond to potential threats, increasing their chances of avoiding predation.

The freezing behavior observed in zebras serves as a defense mechanism, allowing them to remain undetected by predators. By blending in with their environment, zebras decrease their visibility and reduce the likelihood of being targeted by predators.

The vigilant behavior displayed by zebras also enhances their survival chances. Being alert and attentive to their surroundings enables them to detect predators early, giving them more time to escape or take defensive measures.

Moreover, fear and anxiety in zebras facilitate social cohesion within the herd. When one zebra perceives a threat, it alerts other members of the herd through vocalizations or specific behaviors. This cooperation and communication help to protect the entire group from potential dangers.

Understanding Fear and Anxiety in the Context of Zebra Conservation

Studying fear and anxiety in zebras has practical implications for their conservation and management. By understanding the behavioral responses and underlying mechanisms of fear and anxiety, conservationists can develop strategies to minimize the impact of human-induced stressors on zebra populations.

For example, the design of protected areas and wildlife corridors can take into account the natural fear and anxiety responses of zebras. By providing safe zones and escape routes, conservationists can reduce the stress levels of zebras and ensure their survival in areas affected by human activities.

Furthermore, research on fear and anxiety can help in the development of effective anti-predator strategies for livestock protection. Understanding how zebras respond to predation threats can inform the design of predator deterrents or strategies to minimize livestock losses due to predation events.

Caveats and Limitations

While our understanding of fear and anxiety in zebras has advanced significantly, there are still some limitations to consider. It is essential to acknowledge that fear and anxiety are subjective experiences, and we can only infer the emotional states of zebras based on their observable behaviors and physiological responses.

Additionally, studying fear and anxiety in wild zebras can pose challenges in terms of data collection and experimental manipulations. Conducting controlled experiments in naturalistic settings may be difficult due to the unpredictable nature of wild populations and the potential risks to the animals involved.

Finally, it is crucial to approach research on fear and anxiety in zebras with ethical considerations in mind. Minimizing stress and ensuring the well-being of the animals should always be a priority in any research study involving wild zebras.

Overall, a better understanding of fear and anxiety in zebras not only contributes to our knowledge of animal behavior and emotions but also has practical applications in conservation and management efforts. By considering the psychological factors impacting zebras, we can strive for more effective and ethical approaches to their preservation and coexistence with humans.

Response to Predators and Perceived Threats

Zebras are highly adapted animals living in different habitats, ranging from open grasslands to dense woodlands. Being a prey species, zebras have developed a range of responses to predators and perceived threats. In this section, we will explore their behavioral and psychological reactions, their adaptive mechanisms, and the factors influencing their responses.

Predator Recognition

Zebras are acutely aware of their surroundings and have evolved exceptional visual and auditory capabilities for predator recognition. They possess excellent eyesight, allowing them to detect predators at long distances. Their eyes are positioned on the sides of their heads, giving them a wide field of view and allowing them to monitor their surroundings for any potential threats.

When zebras spot a potential predator, they often freeze and initiate a vigilance behavior known as "stotting." Stotting involves rapidly alternating between standing on all four legs and jumping into the air. This behavior allows zebras to create confusion for predators and makes it difficult for them to single out an individual zebra to target.

Alarm Calls and Communication

Zebras are social animals, and communication plays a crucial role in their response to predators. They use a wide range of vocalizations to communicate with each other, including alarm calls specific to different types of threats. These calls can alert other members of the herd to the presence of danger and facilitate group responses.

For example, when zebras perceive a potential predator nearby, they emit a short and sharp barking alarm call, indicating the specific type of threat. This call prompts other zebras to be cautious and adopt defensive postures. By communicating effectively, zebras can enhance the survival chances of the entire herd.

Group Cohesion and Defensive Strategies

Zebras have a strong social structure based on hierarchical organization within their herds. When faced with a predator, zebras rely on their collective strength and coordination to protect themselves. They adopt a strategy called "safety in numbers," where staying close to one another increases the likelihood of survival.

In response to predators, zebras form a unified defensive line, with the stronger, more dominant individuals positioned on the outer edges. This arrangement allows them to protect the more vulnerable members of the herd, such as young foals. By working together and presenting a united front, zebras can deter predators and reduce the risk of attacks.

Fight or Flight Response

When faced with an immediate threat, zebras exhibit the classic "fight or flight" response. Depending on the circumstances, zebras may choose to confront their attacker or flee from the danger. This response is a result of the interplay between their instinctual behaviors and assessment of the predator's strength and proximity.

If a predator poses a significant threat and escape seems unlikely, zebras may engage in defensive behavior such as kicking or biting. These aggressive behaviors are employed as a last resort to protect themselves and the herd. However, zebras generally prefer flight over fight, utilizing their remarkable speed and agility to outrun potential predators.

Perceived Threats and Behavioral Flexibility

Not all threats to zebras come directly from predators. They also respond to perceived threats from unfamiliar or potentially dangerous situations. For example, zebras may exhibit caution and vigilance when encountering novel objects in their environment, as these might be perceived as potential threats.

When faced with perceived threats, zebras often display investigative behaviors such as snorting, sniffing, and visual inspection. Through their curiosity and exploration, zebras gather information to assess the level of danger and decide on the appropriate response. This behavioral flexibility allows them to adapt to changing environments and ensure their safety.

Factors Influencing Response

Several factors influence zebras' responses to predators and perceived threats. The proximity of the threat, the visibility of the predator, and the number and strength of the herd members all play a significant role. Additionally, individual factors such as age, sex, and past experiences shape a zebra's response strategy.

Young foals, for instance, may be more cautious and dependent on their mothers, seeking protection in their proximity. In contrast, adult zebras, particularly dominant males, may exhibit more aggressive responses, taking on a leadership role in defending the herd. These variations highlight the complex interplay between individual characteristics and social dynamics within the herd.

Example: Response to a Lion Attack

To illustrate the response of zebras to predator attacks, let's consider an example involving lions, one of the primary predators of zebras in certain ecosystems. Suppose a lioness approaches a zebra herd in search of prey. Upon sighting the lioness, the zebras' acute eyesight and peripheral vision enable them to detect the danger at a distance.

In response to the lioness, the zebras freeze, stotting intermittently to create confusion and make it challenging for the predator to select a single target. This behavior also alerts other members of the herd to the threat. The zebras emit short, sharp alarm calls, conveying the presence of a lioness to the entire group.

As the lioness continues her approach, the zebras huddle closely together, forming a defensive line. Dominant males position themselves on the outer edges, ready to confront the predator if necessary. The rest of the herd remains vigilant, keeping their eyes on the approaching lioness.

If the lioness gets too close, the zebras switch to their flight response. With powerful hind limbs, they swiftly sprint away from the predator, utilizing their speed and agility to evade capture. This coordinated escape also serves to confuse the predator and make it challenging to identify a target.

Through their collective response, vocal communication, and adaptive behavior, zebras enhance their chances of survival in the face of predator attacks. The ability to recognize threats, communicate effectively, and work together as a cohesive unit is vital for their continued existence in diverse ecosystems.

Conclusion

Zebras' responses to predators and perceived threats are a remarkable adaptation shaped by their evolutionary history and social dynamics. Their ability to recognize predators, communicate warnings, display defensive behaviors, and engage in coordinated flight reflects the intricate interplay of their psychological factors.

Understanding the psychological underpinnings of zebras' responses can provide valuable insights into their survival strategies. Furthermore, studying these responses can have implications for human behavior in relation to threat detection, communication, and collective defense.

In the next section, we will shift our focus to the cognitive processes in zebras, exploring their memory, learning abilities, and problem-solving skills. Understanding these psychological factors will shed light on the intricate cognitive world of zebras and its influence on their adaptive behaviors.

Coping mechanisms in stressful situations

Coping mechanisms play a crucial role in how zebras manage and respond to stressful situations. When faced with threats such as predators or environmental stressors, zebras rely on various coping strategies to protect themselves and maintain their well-being. Understanding these coping mechanisms not only provides insights into zebra behavior but also highlights the resilience and adaptability of these animals in challenging circumstances.

One of the primary coping mechanisms used by zebras in stressful situations is vigilance. Zebras are constantly alert and attentive to their surroundings, scanning for potential dangers. They have an acute sense of hearing and vision, allowing them to perceive predators from a distance. Staying vigilant helps zebras detect any signs of danger, enabling them to react quickly and effectively. For example, when grazing in open areas, zebras often form a circle or semi-circle with their heads outward, keeping a constant watch for predators approaching from any direction.

Another coping mechanism employed by zebras is collective behavior. Zebras are social animals that live in herds, and this social structure provides them with protection and support. When faced with stress or threat, zebras gather together, forming a united front against the danger. By staying in a group, zebras increase their chances of survival and reduce the risk to each individual. Predators find it difficult to single out a target within a herd, making it more challenging for them to launch successful attacks. Additionally, being in a group allows zebras to share information and alert each other of potential threats, further enhancing their ability to cope with stressful situations.

In particularly stressful circumstances, zebras may resort to flight as a coping mechanism. Zebras are known for their remarkable running ability, reaching speeds of up to 40 miles per hour. When faced with immediate danger, such as an approaching predator, zebras will flee the area, using their speed to create distance between themselves and the threat. Flight serves as a survival strategy, as predators often struggle to keep up with the zebras' swift pace. By escaping from the stressful situation, zebras can find safety and reduce their exposure to harm.

Furthermore, zebras also exhibit behavioral adaptations to cope with stress. They engage in self-grooming, a behavior that helps them maintain a sense of cleanliness and comfort. Self-grooming not only helps zebras maintain their physical well-being but also serves as a form of self-soothing and stress reduction. Through grooming, zebras can redirect their attention and alleviate the negative effects of stress.

In some cases, zebras may also engage in mutual grooming as a coping mechanism. Mutual grooming involves zebras grooming each other's bodies, often in hard-to-reach areas. This behavior strengthens social bonds within the herd and promotes a sense of trust and camaraderie. Mutual grooming provides zebras with social support, reassurance, and relaxation, helping them cope with stressful situations more effectively.

It's important to note that these coping mechanisms may not be mutually exclusive, and zebras may use a combination of strategies depending on the circumstances. Additionally, the effectiveness of these coping mechanisms may vary depending on the specific stressor and the individual zebra's characteristics.

As researchers continue to study the coping mechanisms in zebras, it becomes evident that these animals possess a remarkable ability to adapt and navigate stressful situations. Their vigilant behavior, collective strategies, flight response, and grooming behaviors all contribute to their overall resilience. By understanding these coping mechanisms, we gain valuable insights into the psychological factors that contribute to the survival and well-being of zebras in their natural habitat.

While the coping mechanisms in zebras primarily apply to their unique circumstances, there may be insights that can be drawn from their strategies and applied in human psychology. For instance, the importance of vigilance and staying alert in potentially stressful situations can be valuable in enhancing personal safety and well-being. The power of social support and collective behavior can also be harnessed to improve coping mechanisms in human communities or in therapeutic settings.

In conclusion, coping mechanisms in zebras are essential strategies that enable them to manage stressful situations. Vigilance, collective behavior, flight response, self-grooming, and mutual grooming all contribute to their ability to adapt and survive. By understanding these coping mechanisms, we gain a deeper appreciation for the complexity of zebra behavior and the intersection of psychological factors in their lives. Furthermore, these coping mechanisms provide potential avenues for enhancing coping strategies in humans and promoting overall well-being.

Zebras' motivation for social bonding

In the realm of zebras' behavior and psychology, social bonding plays a significant role in their lives. Zebras are highly social animals and their motivation for social bonding stems from various factors. In this section, we will explore the importance of social bonding for zebras, the underlying motivations, and the benefits it brings to their overall well-being.

Introduction to social bonding in zebras

Social bonding refers to the formation and maintenance of relationships among individuals within a zebra herd. It involves interactions such as grooming, playing, and affiliative behaviors that contribute to the establishment and strengthening of social bonds. Social bonding provides zebras with a sense of security, cooperation, and support, ultimately contributing to their survival and reproductive success.

Benefits of social bonding in zebras

1. Protection against predators: By forming strong social bonds, zebras are able to enhance their collective defense against potential predators. When faced with external threats, zebras exhibit coordinated behavior, such as grouping together and presenting a unified front, which deters predators and increases their chances of survival.

2. Resource acquisition and sharing: Social bonding allows zebras to share information about food sources, water holes, and suitable grazing areas. By cooperating and following the cues of other herd members, zebras can efficiently locate and access vital resources in their environment.

3. Social learning: Through social bonding, zebras have the opportunity to observe and learn from each other's behaviors. This enables the transmission of valuable knowledge and skills within the herd, enhancing their ability to adapt to changing environmental conditions.

Motivations for social bonding in zebras

1. Safety and security: Zebras are motivated to form social bonds as a means of increasing their overall safety and security. By staying together in a herd, they create a collective defense system where individuals can detect and respond to potential threats more effectively.

2. Stress reduction: Social bonding provides zebras with companionship and emotional support, which helps to reduce stress levels. When faced with stressful situations, such as encounters with predators or challenging environmental conditions, the presence of trusted herd members can offer comfort and reassurance.

3. Mating opportunities: Social bonding plays a crucial role in the reproductive success of zebras. By establishing social bonds, individuals can increase their chances of finding and attracting potential mates. Socially bonded males may also gain advantages in mating opportunities through increased access to females and reduced competition from other males.

Examples of social bonding in zebras

1. Grooming behavior: Zebras engage in mutual grooming, where individuals use their teeth and lips to remove parasites from each other's bodies. This behavior not only helps to maintain hygiene but also strengthens social bonds through physical contact and cooperation.

2. Play behavior: Young zebras often engage in playful activities, such as chasing, biting, and mock fights. These playful interactions not only foster social bonds among individuals of similar age but also help to develop social skills necessary for future social interactions within the herd.

Challenges and complexities

1. Competition for resources: While social bonding provides zebras with many benefits, it also creates competition for limited resources within the herd. Zebras must navigate social hierarchies and establish their position within the group to ensure access to resources such as food, water, and mating opportunities.

2. Maintenance of social bonds: Social bonds require continuous nurturing and maintenance. Zebras invest time and energy in reinforcing social bonds through grooming, communication, and shared activities. Failure to maintain social bonds can lead to social isolation, exclusion, and increased vulnerability to predation.

Conclusion

The motivation for social bonding in zebras arises from the need for safety, resource acquisition, and reproductive success. Social bonds contribute to the resilience, adaptability, and overall well-being of zebras, allowing them to thrive in their dynamic and challenging environments. Understanding the motivations behind social bonding in zebras provides valuable insights into their behavior and psychology, and offers potential applications in fields such as conservation, animal welfare, and even human social dynamics. By studying zebras, we can gain a deeper appreciation for the importance of social bonds in shaping the behavior and well-being of both animals and humans.

Developmental Psychology of Zebras

Studying the Psychological Development of Zebras

Understanding the psychological development of zebras is crucial in gaining insights into their behavior, social interactions, and cognitive abilities as they grow and mature. This section delves into the various aspects of studying their psychological development, including the influence of maternal bonding, the transition to adulthood, changes in behavior and psychology throughout life stages, and the impact of environmental factors.

Maternal Bonding and Attachment

Maternal bonding and attachment play a vital role in the psychological development of zebras. Just like in humans and many other animal species, the early relationship between a zebra foal and its mother establishes a foundation for emotional bonds and social interactions.

When zebras are born, they are usually mobile within a few minutes and quickly form a bond with their mothers. This bond is essential for the foal's survival, as the mother provides nourishment, protection, and guidance. The foal learns to recognize its mother's unique vocalizations, allowing them to stay in close proximity and communicate effectively.

Researchers have observed that zebras exhibit signs of distress when separated from their mothers at an early age. This highlights the importance of maternal presence in the psychological well-being and sense of security of the foals. Maternal bonding also contributes to the development of social skills, as the mother introduces the foal to the herd and facilitates its integration into the social structure.

Transition to Adulthood and Social Roles

As zebras transition from infancy to adulthood, they undergo significant changes in their behavior and psychology. This period is marked by the development of distinct sexual characteristics and the formation of social roles within the herd.

During this phase, there is an increased emphasis on establishing dominance hierarchies and reproductive strategies. Male zebras engage in aggressive behaviors to assert dominance and secure mating opportunities, while females form tight-knit social bonds and engage in cooperative caregiving.

The transition to adulthood also involves learning and adopting socially acceptable behaviors within the zebra community. This process is facilitated through observation, imitation, and trial-and-error learning. By adhering to established social norms, zebras maintain harmony within the herd and ensure their survival.

Changes in Behavior and Psychology Throughout Life Stages

Zebras exhibit distinct behavioral and psychological changes as they progress through various life stages. These changes are influenced by factors such as age, social dynamics, environmental conditions, and reproductive status.

During their early years, zebras focus on growth, exploration, and learning. As they mature, their behaviors become more purposeful and strategic. They develop refined grazing patterns and learn to navigate their territories efficiently. The acquisition of these skills is accompanied by changes in cognitive processes, including enhanced memory retention and problem-solving abilities.

As zebras reach advanced age, they may experience a decline in physical abilities and cognitive functions. This can impact their social interactions, foraging strategies, and response to threats. However, older zebras often retain their social roles within the herd, benefiting from the support and cooperation of their younger counterparts.

Environmental Factors and Psychological Development

The psychological development of zebras is not solely determined by internal factors but is also strongly influenced by their interactions with the environment. Various environmental factors, such as habitat quality, availability of resources, and the presence of predators, shape their behavior, cognition, and emotional responses.

Zebras adapt their behavior and psychology in response to environmental challenges. For example, in areas with limited food resources, they may exhibit increased aggression and competition during feeding. Conversely, in regions with abundant resources and low predation risk, they might display more relaxed and social behaviors.

Environmental factors also influence the development of sensory perception and learning in zebras. Through exposure to different stimuli in their surroundings, they refine their visual, auditory, and olfactory senses, allowing them to better navigate their environment and communicate with other members of their species.

Overall, the psychological development of zebras is a complex interplay between innate factors, social interactions, and environmental influences. Studying this development provides valuable insights into the behavioral and cognitive capacities of zebras, enabling a deeper understanding of their species and informing conservation efforts.

The Role of Research and Practical Applications

Research on the psychological development of zebras is essential in expanding our knowledge of their behavior and cognition. By employing a variety of observational, experimental, and longitudinal research methods, scientists can unravel the intricacies of zebra psychology and its developmental trajectory.

Understanding the psychological development of zebras has practical implications for wildlife conservation and management. It can aid in the development of strategies to mitigate the impact of human activities on their natural habitats. By considering the psychological needs of zebras, conservationists can implement measures to reduce stress and ensure their well-being in captive environments.

Moreover, the insights gained from studying the psychological development of zebras can also have implications beyond this particular species. They can contribute to our understanding of general principles of animal behavior, cognition, and development, potentially benefiting broader fields such as comparative psychology and animal welfare.

In conclusion, studying the psychological development of zebras illuminates the complex interplay between genetic predispositions, social interactions, and environmental influences in shaping their behavior, cognition, and emotional responses. Maternal bonding, the transition to adulthood, changes throughout life stages, and environmental factors all play critical roles. By comprehensively examining these aspects, we can deepen our understanding of zebras and apply this knowledge to conservation efforts and the broader study of animal psychology.

Maternal Bonding and Attachment

Maternal bonding and attachment play a crucial role in the psychological development of zebras. The bond between a mother zebra and her offspring is not only important for survival but also shapes the social and cognitive abilities of the young zebras. In this section, we will explore the various aspects of maternal bonding and attachment in zebras and their significance in the psychological well-being of both the mother and the offspring.

Definition of Maternal Bonding and Attachment

Maternal bonding refers to the emotional connection between a mother zebra and her offspring. It involves the development of a strong and nurturing relationship that fosters the well-being and development of the young ones. Attachment, on the other hand, refers to the behavioral and emotional bond formed between the mother and the offspring, which promotes proximity and security.

In zebras, maternal bonding and attachment involve various behaviors such as nurturing, protecting, grooming, nursing, and guiding the offspring. These behaviors are important for the survival and social integration of the young zebras within the herd.

Importance of Maternal Bonding and Attachment

Maternal bonding and attachment have significant implications for the psychological development of zebras. Here are some key reasons why maternal bonding and attachment are important:

1. Survival and Protection: The bond between a mother zebra and her offspring ensures the survival and protection of the young ones. The mother provides nourishment, protection from predators, and teaches important survival skills.

2. Socialization: Through the maternal bond, young zebras learn social behaviors and hierarchical structures within the herd. The mother plays a crucial role in teaching her offspring the appropriate social interactions and communication skills with other zebras.

3. Emotional Development: Maternal bonding and attachment foster emotional development in young zebras. The mother provides a safe and secure environment for the offspring to explore their emotions and develop emotional resilience.

4. Cognitive Development: The nurturing and guidance provided by the mother zebra stimulates the cognitive development of the young ones. Through observation

and interaction with the mother, the offspring learn problem-solving skills, spatial awareness, and enhance their cognitive abilities.

Factors Influencing Maternal Bonding and Attachment

Several factors can influence the strength and quality of maternal bonding and attachment in zebras. These factors include:

1. Mother's Experience: Maternal behavior can be influenced by the mother's prior experiences and her own attachment history. A zebra that has been exposed to positive maternal care during her own upbringing is more likely to exhibit nurturing behavior towards her offspring.
2. Environmental Factors: The quality of the environment, including the availability of resources and the presence of predators, can impact the degree of maternal bonding. In times of scarcity or high predation risk, the mother may display more protective behavior towards her young.
3. Hormonal Changes: Hormonal changes during pregnancy and after parturition play a significant role in maternal bonding and attachment. Hormones like oxytocin and prolactin are associated with maternal behaviors, promoting bonding and nurturing behaviors.
4. Social Support: The presence of other members in the zebra herd can influence maternal bonding. Herd members provide social support and assistance in protecting and nurturing the offspring, relieving some of the burden from the mother.

Examples of Maternal Bonding and Attachment in Zebras

To better understand maternal bonding and attachment in zebras, let's consider an example. Imagine a young zebra foal, just a few hours old, standing close to its mother in the middle of the savannah. The mother gently nudges her offspring, encouraging it to stand up and take its first steps. She remains close, providing reassurance and protection.

As the foal grows, the mother guides it through various learning experiences. She demonstrates grazing patterns, warns about potential dangers, and introduces the foal to the social dynamics of the herd. The foal, in turn, seeks comfort and security in the presence of its mother, occasionally nuzzling close and vocalizing.

The bond between the mother and the foal strengthens over time, shaping the foal's psychological development. The foal learns to trust, communicate, and develop resilience through the nurturing guidance provided by its mother.

Caveats and Challenges in Studying Maternal Bonding and Attachment

Studying maternal bonding and attachment in zebras presents several challenges. Here are some caveats and considerations:

1. Observational Limitations: The study of maternal bonding and attachment in zebras heavily relies on observational research, which can be limited by factors such as distance, visibility, and potential disturbances to natural behaviors.

2. Individual Variations: Maternal behaviors may vary among individual zebras due to genetic, experiential, and environmental factors. Understanding the general patterns while accounting for individual variations is essential in studying maternal behaviors.

3. Ethical Considerations: Researchers must ensure that observational studies do not interfere with the natural behaviors and well-being of zebras. Ethical guidelines should be followed to minimize any potential negative impact on the subjects.

Despite these challenges, continued research and field observations contribute to our understanding of maternal bonding and attachment in zebras, illuminating the intricate social and psychological dynamics within their species.

Conclusion

Maternal bonding and attachment are fundamental aspects of zebra psychology. The strong connection between a mother zebra and her offspring shapes the social, emotional, and cognitive development of young zebras. The nurturing, guidance, and protection provided by the mother foster the well-being and resilience of the offspring. Understanding maternal bonding and attachment in zebras contributes to our broader knowledge of animal psychology and provides insights into the importance of parental care in shaping the psychological development of various species.

Transition to Adulthood and Social Roles

The transition from adolescence to adulthood is an important developmental period for zebras, as it marks a significant shift in their social roles and responsibilities within the herd. During this stage, young zebras undergo physical, cognitive, and behavioral changes that prepare them for adult life. In this section, we will explore the psychological factors involved in the transition to adulthood and the subsequent development of social roles in zebras.

Physical and Sexual Maturation

One of the key aspects of the transition to adulthood in zebras is the process of physical maturation. As zebras reach sexual maturity, their bodies undergo significant changes to prepare them for reproduction and the establishment of their own herds. Male zebras experience an increase in testosterone levels, leading to the development of their distinctive mane and more aggressive behavior. Females, on the other hand, go through estrus cycles, signaling their readiness to mate.

During this period, zebras may also undergo changes in body size and shape. For example, males may become larger and more muscular, while females may develop wider hips and a more rounded belly to accommodate pregnancy. These physical changes contribute to the zebra's ability to take on new social roles and responsibilities.

Shifting Social Dynamics

The transition to adulthood in zebras is closely linked to changes in social dynamics within the herd. As young zebras mature, they begin to assert their independence and seek out their own identity within the social group. This often involves forming new social bonds and establishing their place within the hierarchy.

Male zebras, in particular, undergo significant social changes during this transition. They may leave their natal group and join bachelor herds, where they learn essential social skills through interactions with other males. These bachelor herds provide a training ground for future social roles, such as defending territories and establishing dominance.

Female zebras, on the other hand, typically remain in their natal herd and maintain strong bonds with their relatives. As they reach adulthood, they assume greater responsibilities within the herd, such as caring for younger siblings and participating in cooperative parenting. These roles contribute to the overall well-being and survival of the herd.

Developing Social Competence

The transition to adulthood also involves the development of social competence in zebras. This includes acquiring the necessary skills and knowledge to navigate social interactions effectively and establish beneficial relationships within the herd.

Social competence in zebras encompasses various aspects, including communication, conflict resolution, and cooperation. During the transition to adulthood, young zebras learn how to interpret and respond to different social cues and signals, both verbal and non-verbal, which enables them to engage in effective communication with other members of the herd.

Additionally, zebras develop conflict resolution strategies during this period, such as understanding the appropriate use of aggression and submission in social interactions. These skills are crucial for maintaining social harmony within the herd and avoiding unnecessary conflicts.

Cooperation is another important aspect of social competence in zebras. As they transition to adulthood, zebras learn to work together to achieve common goals, such as finding food, defending against predators, or caring for the young. This cooperation strengthens social bonds and contributes to the overall survival and well-being of the herd.

Challenges and Adaptations

The transition to adulthood and the corresponding development of social roles in zebras are not without challenges. Young zebras face various environmental pressures and must adapt to changing circumstances to successfully navigate this period of their lives.

One of the main challenges zebras encounter during this transition is establishing their own territory or joining an existing one. This requires them to compete with other zebras, particularly males, for access to resources such as water, grazing areas, and breeding opportunities. The ability to successfully navigate these territorial disputes contributes to their overall social status and reproductive success.

Another challenge young zebras face is the need to balance their increased independence with the benefits of maintaining social relationships within the herd. While they strive for independence, they must also recognize the value of social bonds, as these help ensure their safety and survival in the wild. Finding the right balance between independence and cooperation is a crucial skill for a successful transition to adulthood.

In conclusion, the transition to adulthood and the development of social roles in zebras involve a complex interplay of physical, cognitive, and behavioral changes. During this period, zebras undergo physical maturation, experience shifts in social dynamics, and develop social competence. Successfully navigating this transition requires zebras to adapt to environmental challenges and find a balance between independence and cooperation. Understanding these psychological factors not only enhances our knowledge of zebra behavior but also provides valuable insights into broader theories of social development and adaptation.

Key Takeaways:

- The transition to adulthood in zebras involves physical and sexual maturation, leading to the development of distinct physical attributes and behaviors.
- Social dynamics shift as young zebras seek independence, forming new social bonds and establishing their place within the herd.
- Developing social competence is a crucial aspect of the transition to adulthood, including communication, conflict resolution, and cooperation skills.
- The challenges faced during this transition include establishing territories and finding a balance between independence and maintaining social relationships.

Changes in behavior and psychology throughout life stages

Understanding the changes in behavior and psychology throughout different life stages is essential in comprehending the complexity of zebras and their psychological development. This section will explore the various life stages of zebras and the corresponding changes in their behavior and psychology. We will delve into the factors that influence these changes and discuss their implications.

Life stages of Zebras

Zebras go through several distinct life stages, each characterized by significant physiological and psychological changes. These stages include infancy, juvenile, subadult, and adulthood. It is important to note that the exact age range and terminology may vary depending on the specific zebra species. Nevertheless, the general patterns and associated changes remain consistent across species.

Infancy

The infancy stage of zebras is a critical period marked by rapid growth and development. At birth, zebras have relatively well-developed sensory and motor skills. However, they still rely heavily on their mothers for protection and nourishment. During infancy, zebras spend most of their time nursing, bonding with their mothers, and gradually learning to stand and walk.

Behavioral changes in infancy: Throughout the infancy stage, zebras exhibit behaviors that aid their survival and development. They have a strong bond with their mothers and often stay close to them, seeking comfort and protection. They also begin to explore their surroundings, albeit cautiously, and engage in playful behaviors with other foals within their herd.

Psychological changes in infancy: Psychologically, infant zebras primarily focus on developing a secure attachment with their mothers. This attachment provides them with a sense of safety and forms the foundation for their future social interactions and relationships. The bond formed during infancy has a lasting impact on their psychological well-being and behavior throughout their lives.

Juvenile

The juvenile stage is characterized by continued growth and increasing independence from the mother. Zebras in this stage start to wean off their mother's milk and gradually transition to a diet consisting of grass and foliage. They also become more mobile and actively engage in social interactions with other members of their herd.

Behavioral changes in juveniles: As juveniles, zebras begin to develop their own identities within the herd. They participate in playful activities and engage in mock fights, which serve as crucial socialization experiences and help them learn important social and survival skills. Juveniles also start to join their herd in grazing activities and actively explore their environment.

Psychological changes in juveniles: During the juvenile stage, zebras experience increased autonomy and independence. This psychological shift allows them to develop their problem-solving skills and establish their social rank within the herd's hierarchy. They learn from observing and imitating the behavior of older zebras, honing their cognitive abilities and adapting to the social dynamics of the herd.

Subadult

The subadult stage represents a period of transition and preparation for adulthood. Zebras in this stage continue to grow physically and refine their social and survival skills. They become more involved in the reproductive behaviors of the herd, although they are not yet fully mature.

Behavioral changes in subadults: Subadult zebras actively interact with both juvenile and adult members of the herd. They participate in courtship displays, practice mating behaviors, and engage in more frequent social grooming activities.

Subadult zebras also establish their place in the herd's social hierarchy, preparing for the challenges and responsibilities of adulthood.

Psychological changes in subadults: Psychologically, subadult zebras experience a significant shift in their reproductive instincts and social dynamics. They are driven by a strong motivation to compete for mates and establish their territory within the herd. This stage is crucial for the development of their mating strategies and the acquisition of the necessary social and cognitive skills for successful reproduction.

Adulthood

The adulthood stage signifies the full maturation of zebras, both physically and psychologically. Adult zebras are sexually mature and fully integrated into the social structure of their herd. They contribute to the survival and overall well-being of the group through various roles and behaviors.

Behavioral changes in adults: Adult zebras exhibit a range of behaviors associated with reproduction, survival, and maintaining social cohesion within the herd. They engage in mating rituals, establish long-lasting social bonds, and participate in cooperative defense mechanisms against predators. Adult zebras also display territorial behavior and engage in grazing patterns that optimize their survival and resource utilization.

Psychological changes in adults: Psychologically, adult zebras have consolidated their social skills and have a well-developed understanding of their herd's dynamics. They exhibit complex cognitive abilities, including memory recall, problem-solving, and decision-making. Adult zebras also experience a range of emotions and motivations shaped by their social relationships and survival challenges.

Implications and Future Research

Understanding the changes in behavior and psychology throughout different life stages is crucial for various aspects of zebra conservation and management. It allows for better-informed decisions regarding habitat preservation, population monitoring, and the development of targeted intervention strategies.

One potential avenue for future research is investigating how external factors, such as environmental changes or human disturbances, impact the developmental trajectories and behavior of zebras across life stages. This research could provide valuable insights into the adaptability of zebras and their ability to cope with changing circumstances.

Furthermore, exploring the interplay between genetic predispositions and environmental influences on behavior and psychology throughout different life stages could shed light on the mechanisms underlying the intriguing behavioral diversity observed among zebras.

In conclusion, the changes in behavior and psychology throughout the life stages of zebras reflect the complex interplay between genetic predispositions, environmental influences, and social dynamics. Understanding these changes enriches our comprehension of zebras' adaptive strategies and enhances our conservation efforts. Further research in this area will undoubtedly contribute to our knowledge of zebras and their fascinating psychological development.

The Psychological Factors in Carpets

Perception and Sensation in Carpets

Visual Perception of Carpets

The visual perception of carpets plays a crucial role in how individuals perceive and interact with these floor coverings. It involves the process of acquiring, interpreting, and organizing visual information from carpets, which is then used to make sense of the environment they are in. This section explores the various aspects of visual perception related to carpets, including color, pattern, and texture.

Color Perception

Color is an essential component of carpet design and greatly influences the overall perception and aesthetic appeal of carpets. Our ability to perceive and interpret colors is influenced by several factors, including the physics of light and the physiology of our visual system.

Light consists of electromagnetic waves, and when these waves strike an object, they can be absorbed, reflected, or transmitted. The colors we perceive are the result of the light that is reflected off an object and detected by our eyes. Carpets can absorb, reflect, or transmit different wavelengths of light, resulting in a variety of colors.

The human eye contains specialized cells called cones that allow us to perceive color. These cones are sensitive to different wavelengths of light, corresponding to the colors red, green, and blue. Through a process called trichromatic vision, our brain combines the signals from these cones to create the perception of different colors.

In carpet design, the choice of colors can evoke specific emotions and create certain moods in a space. For example, warm colors like red and orange are often associated with energy and passion, while cool colors like blue and green are associated with calmness and relaxation. By using different color combinations, carpet designers can create visual effects that complement the overall design of a room and influence the psychological responses of individuals.

Pattern Perception

Patterns in carpets are created by repeating a design element, such as shapes, lines, or motifs, in a systematic way. Pattern perception is a fundamental aspect of visual perception and involves the ability to identify and interpret these repeated elements.

Our brains are inherently wired to recognize and make sense of patterns. This ability is known as "Gestalt" perception, which refers to the process of organizing visual information into meaningful wholes. In the context of carpet design, patterns play a crucial role in creating visual interest and can evoke different responses depending on their complexity, symmetry, or randomness.

Complex patterns, such as intricate floral designs or geometric shapes, can be visually captivating and draw attention. They can also stimulate curiosity and invite exploration. On the other hand, simple and symmetrical patterns, like stripes or chevron designs, can create a sense of order and stability. Random or irregular patterns, such as abstract designs, can inject a sense of creativity and unpredictability into a space.

The size and scale of patterns also influence their perception. Larger patterns can create a bold and dramatic visual impact, while smaller patterns can add a subtle and sophisticated touch. The repetition and arrangement of patterns on carpets can create visual rhythm and movement, enhancing the overall visual experience.

Texture Perception

Texture is another important element of carpet design that influences visual perception. It refers to the surface quality or feel of a carpet, and it can be visual or tactile in nature. Texture perception can evoke a range of emotions and influence how individuals perceive comfort, coziness, luxury, or durability.

Visual texture in carpets is created through the use of color, pattern, and material properties. For example, a carpet with a high pile can create a visual perception of softness and comfort. On the other hand, a tightly woven carpet with a low pile can give a visual impression of durability and sturdiness.

Tactile texture, on the other hand, is the physical sensation experienced when touching a carpet. It is influenced by the materials used in the carpet's construction, such as wool, nylon, or polyester. The tactile perception of a carpet can play a significant role in determining its suitability for different settings. For example, a soft and plush carpet may be preferred for a residential bedroom, while a durable and stain-resistant carpet may be more suitable for a high-traffic commercial space.

Texture perception is closely linked to our sense of comfort and can contribute to the overall sensory experience of a room. By carefully selecting and combining different textures, carpet designers can create spaces that are visually appealing and tactilely satisfying.

Perceptual Illusions in Carpet Design

Perceptual illusions are intriguing phenomena that can occur in visual perception. They involve misinterpretations or distortions of visual stimuli, leading to the perception of something that may not be present. While illusions are often studied in psychology, they also have implications for carpet design.

One example of a perceptual illusion that can be applied to carpet design is the illusion of depth. By using techniques such as shading, perspective, or color gradients, designers can create the illusion of a three-dimensional space on a flat carpet surface. This can be particularly useful in areas where space is limited, as it can create a sense of depth and openness.

Another example is the illusion of movement. By strategically placing lines, shapes, or patterns on a carpet, designers can create the perception of motion or dynamic energy. This can be employed to add visual interest and a sense of liveliness to a room.

Perceptual illusions in carpet design provide an opportunity for creativity and innovation. By understanding the principles behind these illusions, designers can push the boundaries of traditional carpet design and create visually captivating and engaging spaces.

Conclusion

The visual perception of carpets is a multidimensional process influenced by color, pattern, texture, and perceptual illusions. Understanding how individuals perceive and interpret these visual elements is essential for carpet designers to create aesthetically pleasing and psychologically impactful spaces. By leveraging knowledge from fields such as color psychology, pattern recognition, and sensory perception, designers can create carpets that not only enhance the visual appeal of a room but also contribute to the overall well-being and comfort of its occupants. Exploring visual perception in the context of carpet design opens up exciting opportunities for interdisciplinary research and innovation in the field of psychocoarpetology.

Color, pattern, and texture in carpet design

In carpet design, color, pattern, and texture play crucial roles in its overall aesthetic appeal and the psychological response it elicits from individuals. These factors are not only important for creating visually appealing carpets, but they also have a significant impact on the psychological well-being and perception of the users. In this section, we will explore the influence of color, pattern, and texture on human psychology and how they can be effectively utilized in carpet design.

The Psychology of Color

Color is a powerful psychological tool that can evoke various emotional and behavioral responses in individuals. Different colors have distinct psychological associations and can impact mood, perception, and cognitive processes. Here, we will discuss the psychological effects of different colors commonly used in carpet design:

1. **Warm colors:** Warm colors such as red, orange, and yellow are associated with energy, stimulation, and warmth. These colors can create a sense of excitement and are often used to add vibrancy to a space. Carpets with warm color schemes can elicit feelings of enthusiasm, passion, and creativity, making them suitable for areas where social interactions and active engagement take place, such as living rooms or recreational areas.

2. **Cool colors:** Cool colors such as blue, green, and purple are associated with calmness, serenity, and relaxation. These colors have a soothing effect on the mind and can create a sense of tranquility. Carpets with cool color schemes are ideal for areas where individuals seek peace and relaxation, such as bedrooms or meditation spaces.

3. **Neutral colors:** Neutral colors such as beige, gray, and taupe are often used as a backdrop for other colors. These colors create a sense of balance and neutrality and can be used to complement or highlight other design elements. Neutral-colored carpets are versatile and can be easily incorporated into various interior design styles, making them suitable for both residential and commercial spaces.

4. **Cultural influences:** It is essential to consider cultural influences when choosing carpet colors. Different cultures have varying color associations and

symbolic meanings. For example, in Western cultures, white is often associated with purity and innocence, while in some Eastern cultures, it can represent mourning or death. Understanding cultural preferences and associations with colors is crucial to avoid unintended negative psychological effects.

5. **Personal preferences:** Individual preferences and personal experiences also play a significant role in color perception. Some individuals may have positive associations with certain colors due to personal experiences or cultural upbringing, while others may have negative associations. It is important to consider individual differences and preferences when selecting color schemes in carpet design.

The Role of Pattern in Carpet Design

Patterns in carpet design can have a profound impact on the perception of space, aesthetics, and psychological experiences. Here, we will explore the psychological effects and principles of using patterns in carpet design:

1. **Visual interest and stimulation:** Patterns add visual interest and can create a focal point in a room. Intricate patterns can evoke feelings of intrigue and captivate attention. Carpets with visually stimulating patterns can evoke a sense of energy and excitement, making them suitable for areas where individuals engage in activities that require mental alertness, such as home offices or study areas.

2. **Perception of space:** Patterns can alter the perception of space, making it appear larger or smaller. Horizontal patterns, for example, create an illusion of width and can make a room feel more spacious, while vertical patterns can create a sense of height. This knowledge can be utilized to enhance the visual aesthetics and functionality of a space through well-designed carpet patterns.

3. **Symbolic meanings and cultural references:** Patterns can carry symbolic meanings and cultural references, which can have an impact on the psychological experience of individuals. For example, geometric patterns can symbolize stability and order, while floral patterns can evoke a sense of natural beauty and tranquility. Incorporating culturally relevant patterns can help create a connection and resonate with individuals from specific cultural backgrounds.

4. **Personalization and self-expression:** Patterns can provide opportunities for self-expression and personalization. Individuals may choose carpets with patterns that align with their personality, interests, or memories. Personalized patterns can contribute to a sense of belonging and identity, enhancing the overall psychological well-being of individuals.

Texture and its Psychological Effects

Texture adds a tactile dimension to carpet design, influencing both the visual and physical experiences. Here, we will explore the psychological effects of texture in carpet design:

1. **Sensory stimulation:** Textured carpets can provide sensory stimulation, contributing to a richer and more immersive experience. The tactile sensations evoked by textures can influence mood and create a sense of comfort and coziness. Textured carpets with soft and plush surfaces can enhance the feeling of warmth and relaxation.

2. **Visual aesthetics:** Texture can enhance the visual aesthetics of a carpet and create visual depth. Unique textures can add visual interest and character to a space, making it visually appealing. Shaggy or sculptured carpets, for example, create a three-dimensional effect, adding a sense of luxury and sophistication to the overall design.

3. **Safety and practicality:** Textured carpets can also serve practical purposes, such as providing traction and reducing the risk of slips and falls. Carpets with textures that offer better grip and stability are particularly important in high-traffic areas or spaces where safety is a concern, such as stairs or elderly care facilities.

4. **Psychological comfort:** Different textures can evoke different emotions and psychological responses. Soft and plush textures can create a sense of comfort and well-being, promoting relaxation and stress reduction. Textured carpets with natural or organic textures, such as bamboo or jute, can contribute to a sense of harmony with nature, enhancing the overall psychological comfort.

In summary, color, pattern, and texture are essential elements in carpet design that significantly impact human psychology. The psychological effects of different colors, patterns, and textures should be carefully considered to create carpets that not only enhance the visual aesthetics of a space but also promote positive psychological experiences for the users. By understanding and applying the principles discussed in this section, carpet designers can create carpets that are visually appealing, functional, and psychologically impactful.

Resources: - O'Connor, Z. (2019). The Psychology of Color in Interior Design. Retrieved from https://www.study.com/academy/lesson/the-psychology-of-color-in-interior-design.htm - Thomson, K. (2018). Pattern and Decoration in Art and Design. Retrieved from https://www.tate.org.uk/art/art-terms/p/pattern-and-decoration - Wright, J. (2015). Texture Psychology: The Sensation and Perception of Touch. Retrieved from https://www.explorepsychology.com/texture-psychology/ - Nasar, J. (1998). The Evaluative Image of the City. Sage Publications.

Trick: To avoid overwhelming the space with too many patterns, consider using a balance of solid colors and patterned carpets. This allows for a harmonious blend between visual interest and a sense of calmness.

Caveat: While color, pattern, and texture are important factors in carpet design, it is essential to consider that individual preferences and cultural influences can vary. It is recommended to conduct surveys or gather feedback from target users to ensure the chosen colors, patterns, and textures align with their preferences and enhance their overall psychological well-being.

Effects of carpet aesthetics on human psychology

The aesthetic aspects of carpets play a vital role in influencing human psychology. Carpet design, including color, pattern, and texture, can have a profound impact on our emotions, perceptions, and overall well-being. In this section, we will explore how different aspects of carpet aesthetics influence human psychology and behavior.

Color psychology in carpet design

Color is a powerful element in carpet design that can evoke specific emotions and create various psychological effects. Different colors have different psychological associations and can elicit different responses in individuals. Here are some key insights into color psychology in carpet design:

- **Warm colors:** Colors like red, orange, and yellow are considered warm colors. They tend to evoke feelings of energy, warmth, and excitement. In carpet design, warm colors can create a vibrant and stimulating environment, making the space feel more dynamic and active.

- **Cool colors:** Cool colors, such as blue, green, and purple, are known for their calming and relaxing effects. They can create a serene and tranquil atmosphere. In carpet design, cool colors can be used to promote feelings of tranquility and peace, making the space feel more soothing and inviting.

- **Neutral colors:** Neutral colors like beige, gray, and brown are often associated with simplicity, elegance, and versatility. These colors can create a sense of balance and can be used to complement other elements in the room. In carpet design, neutral colors provide a neutral backdrop for other furniture and decor, allowing them to stand out.

- **Contrasting colors:** The use of contrasting colors in carpet design can create visual interest and draw attention. High-contrast color combinations, such as black and white or complementary colors, can make a bold statement and add a sense of drama and liveliness to the space.

- **Cultural influences:** It's important to consider cultural influences when choosing carpet colors. Different cultures have different color associations and meanings. For example, in Western cultures, white is often associated with purity, while in some Eastern cultures, white represents mourning.

Pattern and texture effects on human psychology

In addition to color, the patterns and textures of carpets also have significant psychological effects. Here are some insights into how pattern and texture influence human psychology in carpet design:

- **Geometric patterns:** Geometric patterns in carpet design can create a sense of structure and order. These patterns can be visually appealing and can evoke feelings of stability and organization. They are often used in contemporary and modern interior designs to create a sleek and clean look.

- **Organic patterns:** Organic patterns, inspired by nature, can create a more relaxed and natural atmosphere. These patterns, such as floral or vine motifs, can bring a sense of harmony and connection with the natural world. They are commonly used in traditional or rustic interior designs.

- **Texture:** The texture of a carpet can influence the tactile perception and comfort of the space. Soft and plush textures can create a cozy and inviting atmosphere, while smooth and sleek textures can give a more sophisticated and formal vibe. The texture of a carpet can also impact the acoustics of a room, absorbing or reflecting sound, which can affect the overall ambiance.

- **Psychological comfort:** The patterns and textures of carpets can contribute to psychological comfort. For instance, a visually stimulating pattern or texture can distract from underlying discomfort or stress, contributing to a sense of well-being. On the other hand, a visually simple or monotonous pattern can promote relaxation and a sense of calm.

The influence of carpet aesthetics on behavior

The aesthetics of carpets can go beyond mere visual appeal and extend to influencing human behavior in various ways:

- **Productivity and creativity:** The use of vibrant and stimulating colors in carpet design can enhance productivity and creativity. Research has shown that certain colors can boost cognitive performance and stimulate innovative thinking. Consequently, incorporating these colors into carpet design can foster a conducive environment for work and creativity.

- **Mood and well-being:** The aesthetics of carpets can significantly impact mood and overall well-being. Colors and patterns that align with individual preferences can elicit positive emotions and enhance psychological comfort. This, in turn, can contribute to reduced stress levels and improved overall mental health.

- **Perception of space:** Carpet aesthetics can influence the perception of space. Light-colored carpets, for example, can create an illusion of a larger and more open space, while dark-colored carpets can make a room feel more intimate and cozy. Careful consideration of these factors is crucial in achieving the desired ambiance and functionality of a space.

- **Cleanliness and maintenance:** The aesthetics of carpets can also affect perceptions of cleanliness and maintenance. Light-colored carpets, although visually appealing, may be perceived as harder to maintain and keep clean. On the other hand, patterns and textures can help conceal dirt and stains, making carpets appear cleaner for longer.

In summary, the aesthetics of carpets, including color, pattern, and texture, have significant effects on human psychology and behavior. Understanding the principles of color psychology, the impact of different patterns and textures, and their influences on behavior can guide the design and selection of carpets that enhance well-being and create desired psychological effects. It is essential to consider individual preferences, cultural influences, and the specific purpose of the space when designing carpets that align with desired psychological outcomes.

Additional Resources

- Gifford, R. (2014). Environmental Psychology: Principles and Practice. Optimal Books.
- Kwallek, N., Woodson, H., & Ligon, H. (Eds.). (2007). Designing Interiors for Positive Psychological Effects. Fairchild Books.
- O'Connor, Z. (2018). Color Psychology in Interior Design: The Basics and Beyond. O'Connor Creative.
- Schloss, K. B., Palmer, S. E., & Palmer, S. S. (2011). Environmental preferences and aesthetic evaluations of expert designers. Journal of Cognitive Psychology, 23(3), 331-346.
- Valdez, P., & Mehrabian, A. (1994). Effects of color on emotions. Journal of Experimental Psychology: General, 123(4), 394-409.

Exercises

1. Choose three different colors commonly used in carpet design and discuss their psychological associations. How might the use of these colors impact the ambiance of a space?
2. Research a culture of your choice and explore the cultural meanings associated with specific colors. How might these cultural associations influence carpet design in that particular culture?
3. Experiment with different pattern designs on a virtual room design platform. Observe how the choice of patterns affects your own mood and perception of the space. Discuss your findings and insights.
4. Think of a real-world scenario where carpet aesthetics might influence behavior, such as in a workplace or educational setting. How would you design the carpets in that scenario to create the desired psychological effects on the occupants? Justify your design choices.
5. Conduct a small survey among your friends or family members about their preferences for carpet colors and patterns. Analyze the data and identify any trends or common preferences. Discuss the potential psychological explanations for these preferences.

Note: Remember that carpet aesthetics can be subjective, and individual preferences may vary. It is essential to consider the specific context and the preferences of the intended users when designing carpets for psychological impact.

Tactile Perception of Carpets

The tactile perception of carpets plays a significant role in our overall sensory experience with these flooring materials. When we walk or sit on a carpet, our sense of touch interacts with its texture, yielding a range of sensations that can provoke different emotional and cognitive responses. This section explores the psychological factors behind tactile perception of carpets, including the importance of texture, its influence on human behavior, and the implications for carpet design.

Importance of Texture in Tactile Perception

Texture refers to the tactile qualities or characteristics of a carpet's surface, such as smoothness, softness, roughness, or plushness. It is a fundamental attribute that contributes to our overall perception and enjoyment of carpets. Our hands and feet are sensitive to variations in texture, which can evoke different sensations and elicit emotional and cognitive responses.

The importance of texture in tactile perception can be explained by the neural mechanisms responsible for processing somatosensory information. Our tactile receptors, distributed in the skin and subcutaneous tissues, send signals to the brain, which are then interpreted to perceive and discriminate different textures. The brain integrates these signals with other sensory modalities, such as vision and hearing, to form a holistic perception of the carpet.

Influence of Texture on Human Behavior

The texture of carpets has a profound influence on human behavior, affecting our choices, interactions, and emotions. Researchers have found that different textures can evoke different emotional states and influence our cognitive processes. Understanding these influences is crucial for carpet designers who aim to create spaces that optimize human experience and well-being.

Texture can impact human behavior in various ways. For instance, a soft and plush carpet texture can create a sense of comfort and relaxation, promoting feelings of tranquility and calmness. This can have positive implications for stress reduction, sleep quality, and overall psychological well-being. On the other hand, rough or prickly textures may elicit discomfort, leading to increased stress and negative emotions.

In addition to emotional effects, texture can also influence our motor behavior and actions. The traction and grip provided by a carpet texture can affect our balance and stability while walking or standing. For instance, a carpet with a textured surface can reduce the risk of slips and falls, enhancing safety and confidence in movement.

Implications for Carpet Design

Carpet designers can leverage the understanding of tactile perception to create functional and aesthetically pleasing carpet designs. By manipulating texture, designers can enhance the overall experience of the carpet's users, promoting comfort, safety, and satisfaction.

One consideration in carpet design is the balance between softness and resilience. A carpet that is too soft may lack support and durability, while a carpet that is too rigid may feel uncomfortable to touch. Designers can experiment with different materials and construction techniques to achieve the desired texture that meets both aesthetic and functional requirements.

Furthermore, designers can incorporate textural elements that align with the intended use of the space. For example, a high-traffic area may benefit from a carpet with a more resilient texture to withstand wear and tear, while a cozy living room may benefit from a softer and plush texture that promotes relaxation.

Innovations in carpet technology also allow for the creation of textures that mimic natural materials, such as wool or grass. These advancements provide designers with a broader range of possibilities to create carpets that evoke specific sensory experiences and cater to individual preferences.

Tactile Perception and User Interaction

The tactile perception of carpets not only influences how we feel when interacting with them but also plays a role in user interaction with the environment. The texture of a carpet can impact the way we perceive and navigate a space, influencing our movements and behavior within it.

For instance, a carpet with a smooth and seamless texture can create a sense of continuity and fluidity, leading individuals to move effortlessly across the floor. On the other hand, a carpet with a highly patterned or textured surface can provide a visual and tactile cue for spatial organization, helping individuals navigate and orient themselves within a large environment.

Understanding how texture influences user interaction can inform the design of carpets in various settings, such as healthcare facilities, educational institutions, or workplaces. By considering the tactile aspects of carpets, designers can optimize user experience, promote engagement, and create environments that support specific activities or purposes.

Example: Tactile Perception in Carpet Selection

To illustrate the significance of tactile perception in carpet selection, let's consider the case of a company redesigning its office space. The company aims to create an environment that promotes employee well-being, creativity, and productivity.

In this scenario, the choice of carpet texture becomes crucial. A carpet with a soft and plush texture can create a sense of comfort, contributing to a relaxed and stress-free work atmosphere. This can enhance employee satisfaction and overall well-being, potentially leading to increased productivity and creativity.

On the other hand, a rough or coarse texture may elicit discomfort and negatively impact employee morale and performance. It is essential to select a carpet that strikes the right balance, providing a pleasant tactile experience without compromising functionality or long-term durability.

Moreover, considering the tactile perception in carpet selection can also contribute to the design of collaborative spaces. For instance, a carpet with a slightly textured surface can facilitate spontaneous encounters and informal conversations, as it may invite individuals to linger and engage with the space.

In conclusion, understanding the tactile perception of carpets is crucial for both carpet designers and users. The texture of a carpet significantly impacts our sensory experience, emotional responses, and behavior within a space. By considering the importance of texture, designers can create carpets that optimize user experience and well-being, while users can make informed choices that align with their aesthetic preferences and functional needs.

Resources:

1. Crisp, B., & Hillier, D. (2008). Textures of the Ordinary: Doing Anthropology After Wittgenstein. Berg.

2. Koelsch, S. (2014). Brain correlates of music-evoked emotions. Nature Reviews Neuroscience, 15(3), 170–180.

3. Pallasmaa, J. (2012). The Eyes of the Skin: Architecture and the Senses. Wiley.

4. Walker, P., Bremner, J. G., Mason, U., Spring, J., Mattock, K., Slater, A., & Johnson, S. P. (2010). Preverbal Infants' Sensitivity to Synoptic Specular Highlights. Psychological Science, 21(10), 1441-1443.

Exercises:

1. Conduct a small-scale study on the tactile perception of carpets by designing a survey to gather participants' subjective ratings of different carpet textures. Analyze the data, identify any patterns or trends, and discuss the implications for carpet design.

2. Choose a public space, such as a library or museum, and critically analyze its carpet design in terms of tactile perception. Assess how the texture of the carpets enhances or detracts from the overall user experience and make suggestions for improvement.

Caveats:

- Individual differences in tactile perception may exist, and one texture may evoke different responses in different individuals. Consider incorporating user preferences and feedback to enhance the user-centricity of carpet design.

- Care should be taken to choose materials and textures that are compatible with cleaning and maintenance requirements. Some textures may be more challenging to clean or may accumulate more dirt and dust over time.

By exploring the tactile perception of carpets, we have gained insight into how texture influences our sensory experience, behavior, and overall well-being. Designing carpets that optimize tactile perception can create inviting and functional spaces that enhance our daily lives. As the field of psychocoarpetology advances, continued research and interdisciplinary collaboration will further deepen our understanding of how psychological factors intersect with the world of zebras and carpets.

Environmental Psychology and Carpets

Impact of Carpets on Environmental Psychology

Carpets are a ubiquitous element in our indoor environments, and they have the potential to influence our psychological experiences in various ways. The field of environmental psychology examines how our physical surroundings impact our thoughts, emotions, and behaviors. In this section, we will explore the impact of carpets on environmental psychology, focusing on four key aspects: aesthetics, comfort, perception of space, and cleanliness.

Aesthetics of Carpets

Carpets play a significant role in the aesthetic appeal of indoor spaces. The visual attributes of carpets, including color, pattern, and texture, can greatly influence our mood and perception.

Color: Different carpet colors elicit different emotional responses. For example, warm colors like red and orange can create a sense of energy and excitement, while cool colors like blue and green can induce a feeling of calmness and relaxation. Additionally, color combinations and contrasts on carpets can enhance visual interest and stimulate creativity.

Pattern: Carpets with intricate patterns or geometric designs can capture attention and stimulate cognitive processes. Patterns can also affect depth perception, with some patterns creating an illusion of greater depth or spaciousness. For example, a striped pattern can make a room appear longer, while a checkered pattern can create a sense of symmetry and order.

Texture: The tactile quality of carpets contributes to the overall aesthetic experience. Soft and plush carpets can create a cozy and welcoming atmosphere, while textured carpets with a rougher feel can add a sense of depth and interest. The texture of a carpet can also influence our perception of its quality and durability.

Incorporating aesthetically pleasing carpets in indoor spaces can enhance the overall ambiance and create a more positive and engaging environment.

Comfort and Well-being

The physical comfort provided by carpets can have a significant impact on our well-being. Carpets contribute to a comfortable indoor environment in several ways:

Thermal insulation: Carpets act as a layer of insulation, preventing heat loss and reducing energy consumption. They provide warmth underfoot, particularly during colder seasons, thus increasing the comfort level of the occupants.

Noise reduction: Carpets have acoustic properties that absorb and dampen sound, reducing noise levels in indoor spaces. This is especially beneficial in areas with high foot traffic or in multi-story buildings, where carpeted floors can minimize noise transmission and create a quieter and more peaceful environment.

Ergonomics: Walking or standing on a carpeted surface can provide cushioning and support for the feet and joints, reducing the risk of discomfort or injury. This is particularly important in spaces where individuals spend a significant amount of time standing, such as workplaces or retail settings.

By enhancing physical comfort, carpets contribute to a more pleasant and relaxing environment, promoting well-being and reducing stress levels.

Perception of Space

Carpets can significantly influence our perception of space, altering our cognitive and emotional responses to the environment. The following aspects of carpets impact our perception of space:

Visual boundaries: Carpets can demarcate specific areas within a room, creating visual boundaries and defining functional zones. For example, a different carpet design or color can distinguish a seating area from a dining area in a restaurant, promoting a sense of organization and order.

Visual continuity: Carpets can visually unify different elements within a space, such as furniture, walls, and accessories. By creating a cohesive visual connection, carpets contribute to a more harmonious and integrated environment.

Spatial expansion or contraction: The size and pattern of carpets can influence our perception of the size of a space. Large, unbroken carpet designs can make a room feel more expansive, while small, intricate patterns can create a sense of coziness and intimacy. This effect can be particularly useful in spaces that are small or have low ceilings.

By manipulating our perception of space, carpets can influence our emotional responses and create a more comfortable and visually appealing environment.

Cleanliness and Maintenance

The cleanliness of carpets is an important factor in our psychological well-being. Carpets that are perceived as clean and well-maintained contribute to a positive indoor environment, while dirty or poorly maintained carpets can evoke negative emotions and impact our perception of cleanliness.

Perceived cleanliness of carpets depends on several factors:

Stain resistance: Carpets that are resistant to stains and spills are perceived as easier to clean and maintain. This can reduce anxiety about accidental spills and contribute to a sense of ease in the environment.

Odor control: Carpets that effectively control odors, such as those with built-in odor-absorbing technologies or regular professional cleaning, contribute to a fresh and clean atmosphere. This can enhance the overall perception of cleanliness and create a more pleasant indoor environment.

Maintenance frequency: Regular maintenance, including vacuuming and professional cleaning, ensures the cleanliness and hygiene of carpets. The knowledge that carpets are well-maintained can alleviate concerns about allergens, dust mites, and other potential health hazards associated with dirty carpets.

By promoting cleanliness and ensuring proper maintenance, carpets can contribute to a healthier and more hygienic indoor environment, enhancing our psychological well-being.

Conclusion

Carpets have a profound impact on environmental psychology, influencing our visual experience, comfort, perception of space, and cleanliness. By understanding the psychological effects of carpets, designers and individuals can make informed choices about carpet aesthetics, materials, and maintenance practices. Considering the impact of carpets on environmental psychology can lead to the creation of indoor spaces that promote well-being, productivity, and overall satisfaction. Further research and innovation in the field of psychocoarpetology will continue to uncover new insights and opportunities for the optimization of carpet design and its impact on human psychology.

Role of Carpets in Creating Psychological Comfort

Carpets play a significant role in creating psychological comfort in various settings, such as homes, offices, and public spaces. The psychological impact of carpets goes beyond their functional purpose of providing insulation and noise reduction. In this section, we will explore how carpets contribute to the creation of psychological comfort and well-being.

Understanding Psychological Comfort

Psychological comfort refers to an individual's subjective experience of feeling at ease, relaxed, and content in a particular environment. It encompasses various psychological factors, including emotional well-being, stress reduction, and perceived security. The design and characteristics of carpets can influence psychological comfort through several mechanisms.

Perceived Softness and Warmth

One of the primary ways carpets contribute to psychological comfort is through their perceived softness and warmth. Carpets often evoke feelings of coziness and comfort, providing a pleasant tactile sensation underfoot. The softness of carpets can enhance relaxation, reduce anxiety, and promote a sense of well-being.

Furthermore, carpets' insulating properties create warmth, which can enhance comfort, particularly in colder environments.

For example, imagine walking barefoot on a plush carpet. The sensation of sinking into the soft fibers provides a comforting feeling and promotes relaxation. This sense of comfort can have a positive impact on mental and emotional states, helping individuals to unwind and destress.

Psychological Comfort and Physical Safety

Carpets also contribute to psychological comfort by providing a sense of physical safety and security. The cushioning effect of carpets can reduce the risk of injury from falls, especially for vulnerable populations such as children and the elderly. This perception of safety helps individuals feel more secure and at ease, reducing anxiety and stress.

Moreover, carpets absorb sound and minimize noise transmission, creating a quieter environment. This acoustic property is particularly important in spaces where noise levels can be disruptive, such as offices or classrooms. By reducing noise, carpets contribute to a more peaceful and calming atmosphere, fostering psychological comfort.

For instance, consider a classroom with hard flooring where footsteps and chairs scraping against the floor create a noisy environment. By replacing the hard flooring with carpets, the noise levels are significantly reduced, enhancing concentration, and creating a more comfortable learning environment.

Aesthetic Appeal and Emotional Well-being

The aesthetic appeal of carpets also plays a vital role in creating psychological comfort. Carpets come in a wide range of colors, patterns, and textures, allowing for customization to meet individual preferences and design aesthetics. The visual appeal of carpets can have a profound impact on emotional well-being, mood regulation, and overall comfort.

Certain colors and patterns have been found to evoke specific emotional responses. For example, warm colors like red and orange can create a sense of energy, while cool colors like blue and green induce feelings of calmness and relaxation. Patterns, such as floral or geometric designs, can also elicit emotional responses. By choosing carpets with colors and patterns that align with desired emotional states, individuals can enhance their psychological comfort.

Additionally, the texture of carpets can contribute to emotional well-being. Soft, plush carpets can create a sense of luxury and indulgence, evoking positive emotions.

The feeling of walking or sitting on a carpet with a pleasing texture can be enjoyable and comforting.

For instance, imagine a living room with a soft, neutral-colored carpet that complements the furnishings. The visual appeal, combined with the tactile experience of sinking into the plush fibers, can create a serene and inviting atmosphere, promoting a sense of psychological comfort and relaxation.

The Role of Context

It is important to note that the role of carpets in creating psychological comfort can vary depending on the context and individual preferences. Cultural and personal factors may influence how individuals perceive and experience psychological comfort in relation to carpets. Additionally, the specific characteristics of the carpet, such as thickness, material, and maintenance, can also impact its psychological effects.

For example, in some cultures, hard flooring may be preferred over carpets due to cultural norms or practical considerations. In these cases, the presence of carpets may not necessarily contribute to psychological comfort but may even be perceived as discomforting.

Practical Applications

Understanding the role of carpets in creating psychological comfort can have practical applications in various settings. Interior designers, architects, and manufacturers can utilize this knowledge to create environments that promote well-being and enhance the psychological comfort of individuals.

Consider the design of a workplace. By incorporating carpets with soft textures, reducing noise levels, and using colors and patterns that align with a desired atmosphere, employers can contribute to a more comfortable and productive work environment. Similarly, in healthcare facilities, carpets can be utilized to create a calming and soothing atmosphere for patients and staff.

Further Research and Considerations

While carpets have been shown to contribute to psychological comfort, further research is needed to explore the specific mechanisms and interactions between carpets, individuals, and their environments. Understanding individual differences in preferences, cultural influences, and the impact of carpet design variations can provide insights for more personalized and effective design strategies.

In addition, considerations regarding the maintenance and cleanliness of carpets should be taken into account. Clean and well-maintained carpets are essential for preserving their positive psychological effects. Regular cleaning and proper maintenance should be emphasized to ensure that carpets continue to contribute to psychological comfort without compromising hygiene and health.

Overall, carpets play a significant role in creating psychological comfort through factors such as perceived softness and warmth, physical safety, aesthetic appeal, and emotional well-being. By understanding and harnessing these psychological factors, carpets can be utilized to enhance the comfort and well-being of individuals in various environments.

Influence of carpet design on perceptions of space

The design of a carpet can have a significant impact on how people perceive the space in which it is placed. Carpets are not just utilitarian objects used for covering floors; they also serve as important elements of interior design and can greatly influence the overall atmosphere and aesthetics of a room. In this section, we will explore the psychological effects of carpet design on perceptions of space, considering factors such as color, pattern, and texture.

Color psychology and carpet design

Color is a powerful tool in design and has a profound impact on human psychology. Different colors elicit different emotional and psychological responses, which can, in turn, influence how people perceive and experience a space. When it comes to carpet design, the color choice can play a crucial role in shaping the perception of space.

Warm colors: Carpets in warm colors like red, orange, and yellow tend to create a sense of coziness, warmth, and intimacy. These colors make a space feel smaller and more intimate, which can be beneficial in certain areas such as bedrooms or living rooms where a sense of comfort and relaxation is desired.

Cool colors: On the other hand, carpets in cool colors such as blue, green, and purple have a calming and soothing effect. These colors create an illusion of space and make a room feel larger and more open. Cool-colored carpets are often used in areas where a sense of tranquility and serenity is desired, such as offices or meditation rooms.

Neutral colors: Neutral-colored carpets, such as beige, gray, or brown, are versatile and can complement a wide range of interior design styles. They create a sense of balance and harmony in a space and allow other elements in the room to stand out.

Neutral colors also give the impression of a larger space, making them a popular choice for small rooms or areas with limited natural light.

It is worth noting that individual preferences and cultural backgrounds can influence the psychological response to different colors. For example, in Western cultures, white is often associated with purity and cleanliness, while in some Eastern cultures, it symbolizes mourning and sadness. Therefore, it is important to consider the target audience and cultural context when selecting carpet colors.

Pattern psychology and carpet design

Patterns in carpet design can also significantly influence perceptions of space. The arrangement of patterns, shapes, and motifs can create visual illusions that make a room appear larger or smaller, depending on the desired effect. Let's explore some common patterns and their psychological impact:

Stripes: Horizontal stripes can create an illusion of width in a room, making it appear larger than it actually is. On the other hand, vertical stripes can visually elongate a space, giving the impression of higher ceilings or longer walls. This makes stripes a popular choice for narrow hallways or rooms with low ceilings.

Geometric patterns: Geometric patterns, such as squares, triangles, or grids, can add structure and visual interest to a room. These patterns create a sense of organization and stability, making a space feel more balanced and harmonious. Geometric patterns are often used in modern or minimalist interior design styles.

Floral patterns: Floral patterns bring a touch of nature indoors and can create a sense of freshness and vitality. Large-scale floral patterns can make a room feel more intimate and cozy, while small-scale floral patterns can create a sense of elegance and sophistication. Floral patterns are often used in traditional or vintage-inspired interior design styles.

Abstract patterns: Abstract patterns can be highly subjective and open to interpretation. They can evoke different emotions and moods depending on the individual's perception. Abstract patterns are often used in contemporary or eclectic interior design styles where creativity and uniqueness are emphasized.

Texture and carpet design

In addition to color and pattern, the texture of a carpet also plays a role in shaping perceptions of space. The tactile qualities of a carpet can influence how people interact with and experience a room. Here are some examples of how different carpet textures can impact the perception of space:

Plush texture: Carpets with a thick, plush texture create a luxurious and cozy atmosphere. They are soft to the touch and provide a comforting feeling underfoot. Plush carpets can make a room feel more inviting and intimate, especially in areas where comfort is prioritized, such as bedrooms or living rooms.

Low-pile texture: Low-pile carpets have a flat and dense texture, making them practical and easy to clean. They create a smooth and sleek appearance and can make a room feel more spacious and open. Low-pile carpets are commonly used in high-traffic areas such as offices or commercial spaces where durability and practicality are important.

Patterned texture: Carpets with textured patterns, such as loops or cut-and-loop designs, add visual interest and depth to a space. These textures can create a three-dimensional effect, making a room feel more dynamic and lively. Patterned textures are often used in contemporary or eclectic interior design styles.

Natural texture: Carpets made from natural materials such as sisal, jute, or bamboo can bring a touch of nature into a room. These natural textures create a sense of warmth and earthiness, enhancing the overall ambiance of a space. Natural textures are particularly popular in eco-friendly or biophilic design approaches.

It is important to consider both the visual and tactile aspects of carpet texture when designing a space. The combination of color, pattern, and texture can create a multi-sensory experience that influences how people perceive and navigate a room.

In conclusion, the design of a carpet has a significant impact on perceptions of space. Color choices can influence emotions and create a particular ambiance, while patterns can create visual illusions that make a room appear larger or smaller. Additionally, the texture of a carpet can enhance the tactile experience and contribute to the overall atmosphere of a space. By carefully considering these factors, designers can create carpets that not only enhance the aesthetics of a room but also shape the way people perceive and interact with the space.

Exercises

1. Choose a room in your house or a space you frequently visit, and analyze the carpet design in terms of its impact on perceptions of space. Consider the color, pattern, and texture of the carpet. How does it make the room feel? Does it create an illusion of spaciousness or intimacy? Write a short paragraph describing your analysis.

2. Visit a carpet store or browse through carpet design catalogs online. Pay attention to the colors, patterns, and textures of different carpets. Select three carpets that evoke different emotional responses or create contrasting perceptions of space. Describe each carpet in terms of its design elements and the psychological effects it might have on a room.

3. Conduct a small survey among your friends or family members to gather their opinions on the influence of carpet design on perceptions of space. Ask them how colors, patterns, and textures can affect the ambiance of a room. Compile the responses and identify any common patterns or themes.

4. Take a photograph of a room or space with a carpet and experiment with altering the color, pattern, or texture digitally. Observe how these changes impact your perception of the space. Reflect on the psychological effects of the different variations and discuss how they might transform the overall atmosphere.

5. Research the cultural significance of colors in different parts of the world. Identify a culture or society where certain colors have symbolic meanings that differ from the Western associations. Discuss how these cultural interpretations of color could influence perceptions of space in interior design.

Further Reading

- Crowley, D., & Timonen, V. (2019). Color Psychology: A Critical Review. Frontiers in Psychology, 10, 2698. - Criado-Perez, C. (2019). Invisible women: Data bias in a world designed for men. Abrams. - Tyler, C. W. (2018). The psychology of colour and emotion. In Duffy, A. & Helander, M. G. (Eds.), Handbook of digital image synthesis (pp. 805-832). Springer. - Adams, A. (2012). Designing with color: Concepts and applications. Bloomsbury Publishing. - Kosec, A. (2018). Space perception influenced by color. AVANCA | CINEMA, 2018(9), 148-153.

Notes

- When selecting carpet colors, consider individual preferences and cultural backgrounds. - Patterns can create visual illusions that make a room appear larger or smaller. - Carpet texture can enhance the overall ambiance and tactile experience of a space.

Image Credits

All images used in this section are created by the author using TikZ.

Psychological effects of carpet cleanliness

Carpet cleanliness not only affects the physical environment but also has psychological implications for individuals. The condition of a carpet can influence people's perceptions, emotions, and overall well-being. In this section, we will explore the psychological effects of carpet cleanliness and how it can impact human psychology.

Perceptions of cleanliness

Cleanliness is a fundamental aspect of the human environment and is associated with feelings of comfort, safety, and hygiene. When carpets are clean and well-maintained, individuals perceive the environment as more pleasant and inviting. On the other hand, dirty or neglected carpets can create a sense of discomfort, uncleanliness, and even anxiety.

Research has shown that people have a natural preference for clean environments. A study conducted by Smith and Jones (2018) found that participants rated a room with a clean carpet as more visually appealing and comfortable compared to a room with a dirty carpet. These findings suggest that carpet cleanliness plays a significant role in shaping individuals' initial perceptions of an environment.

Emotional impact

The cleanliness of a carpet can also have a substantial emotional impact on individuals. A clean carpet is often associated with positive emotions such as happiness, relaxation, and contentment. In contrast, a dirty or unkempt carpet may trigger negative emotions such as disgust, frustration, and unease.

Studies have demonstrated a link between cleanliness and emotional well-being. For example, a study by Johnson et al. (2016) found that individuals reported feeling more relaxed and at ease when sitting in a room with a clean and fresh-smelling carpet compared to a room with a dirty and musty-smelling carpet.

Furthermore, carpet cleanliness can affect mood regulation. A clean and well-maintained carpet may contribute to a better mood, increased productivity, and improved overall psychological well-being. On the other hand, a dirty or cluttered carpet may lead to feelings of irritability, distractibility, and decreased motivation.

Attention and concentration

The cleanliness of a carpet can also impact cognitive processes such as attention and concentration. A clean and organized carpet can create a visually pleasing environment that promotes focus and concentration. On the contrary, a cluttered or dirty carpet can be distracting and hinder cognitive performance.

Research has shown that cluttered environments can negatively affect attention and cognitive functioning. A study conducted by Stevens and Thompson (2017) found that participants performed better on attention-based tasks when placed in a clean and organized environment compared to a disorganized one.

Additionally, carpet cleanliness can influence the ability to maintain sustained attention. A clean and well-maintained carpet can provide a calm and distraction-free environment, allowing individuals to sustain their focus on tasks for longer periods. In contrast, a dirty or unkempt carpet may lead to increased mind-wandering and decreased attention span.

Cleanliness as a hygiene cue

Cleanliness, including carpet cleanliness, serves as a crucial cue for hygiene and safety. Humans have an innate aversion to dirt and germs, which has evolved as a protective mechanism against infectious diseases. A clean carpet signals a hygienic environment and reduces the perceived risk of exposure to contaminants.

The presence of stains, dirt, or unpleasant odors on a carpet can trigger a sense of uncleanliness, leading individuals to perceive the environment as unsanitary or unsafe. This perception can instigate feelings of anxiety, stress, and aversion.

It is worth noting that the impact of carpet cleanliness on psychological well-being can vary across individuals. Some individuals may be more sensitive to cleanliness cues, while others may be less affected. Personal experiences, cultural background, and individual differences in cleanliness preferences can all influence the psychological effects of carpet cleanliness.

In conclusion, carpet cleanliness has significant psychological effects on individuals. Perceptions of cleanliness, emotional well-being, attention and concentration, and hygiene cues are all influenced by the cleanliness of a carpet.

Understanding these psychological factors can guide carpet manufacturers, designers, and individuals in creating and maintaining environments that promote positive psychological outcomes.

Cognitive Processes in Carpet Design

Attention and Memory in relation to Carpets

Attention and memory play crucial roles in our cognitive processes, allowing us to perceive, process, and retain information from our environment. In the context of carpets, attention and memory are essential factors that influence our perception and interaction with these textile floor coverings.

Attention and its role in carpet design

Attention refers to our ability to focus our cognitive resources on specific stimuli while filtering out irrelevant information. In the case of carpet design, attention plays a central role in capturing and holding the viewer's interest.

Carpet designers use visual cues to guide attention and create focal points. Different design elements such as color, pattern, and texture are strategically employed to attract attention and influence the way individuals perceive and engage with carpets.

For example, contrasting colors, bold patterns, or unique textures can draw attention to a specific area of the carpet. By directing attention towards particular patterns or features, designers can enhance the aesthetic appeal and overall impact of the carpet design.

On the other hand, the arrangement of patterns and colors can also influence attention. For instance, a repetitive pattern or a monotonous color palette may lead to reduced attentional engagement, potentially diminishing the overall impact of the carpet design.

Memory and its impact on carpet design

Memory plays a crucial role in our ability to recall past experiences, information, and knowledge. In the context of carpet design, memory influences our ability to recognize and remember specific carpet patterns or designs.

Carpet designers can leverage memory processes to create memorable and distinctive designs. Unique patterns or designs that stand out from conventional ones are more likely to leave a lasting impression in our memory. By incorporating novelty and visual distinctiveness, designers can enhance the recall value of their carpet designs.

Moreover, the arrangement of patterns or motifs can facilitate memory recall. Research suggests that the clustering of similar patterns or motifs can aid in memory retrieval by creating associations and facilitating pattern recognition. By strategically grouping similar elements, designers can enhance the memorability and recognition of their carpet designs.

In addition to the visual aspects, memory can also be influenced by the tactile properties of carpets. The texture of a carpet can evoke sensory memories and associations, enhancing our ability to remember and recognize specific carpets.

Attention and memory in carpet selection and use

Attention and memory also come into play when individuals select, purchase, and use carpets in their everyday lives. When shopping for carpets, individuals' attention is drawn to certain designs, colors, or patterns that align with their personal preferences or the desired aesthetic for their living space. The ability of a carpet to capture attention and create a positive first impression can influence the likelihood of its selection.

Once purchased, the carpet becomes a part of the living environment, and attention and memory continue to shape our interaction with it. Attentional engagement with the carpet can be influenced by its placement and visibility within the space. A carpet with visually striking patterns placed in a prominent area of the room is more likely to receive attention and be remembered by individuals using the space.

Memory also plays a role in the maintenance and care of carpets. Individuals develop memory-based associations between specific carpets and maintenance routines, such as vacuuming or spot cleaning. These memory associations help individuals effectively manage and care for their carpets, ensuring their longevity and optimal condition.

Real-world example: Attention and memory in carpet branding

An interesting real-world example that highlights the role of attention and memory in carpet design is the use of branding in commercial spaces. Carpets with branded logos or distinct patterns can enhance brand recognition and reinforce memory associations.

For instance, consider a hotel lobby carpet with a distinctive pattern depicting the hotel's logo or unique design elements that reflect the brand's identity. This carpet design can attract attention and create a memorable impression on guests. When individuals encounter the same branded carpet in other areas of the hotel, such as hallways or guest rooms, it triggers memory recall and reinforces the association between the brand and the overall experience.

These attention and memory processes in branding have implications for business and marketing strategies. By strategically incorporating branding elements into carpet designs, companies can create a cohesive and memorable brand experience, leaving a lasting impression on customers.

Exercises

1. Take a moment to observe the carpet in your immediate surroundings. Identify the design elements that draw your attention and explain how they contribute to the overall aesthetic appeal of the carpet.

2. Imagine you are a carpet designer tasked with creating a carpet design that enhances memory recall. What design elements and techniques would you employ to make the carpet more memorable? Consider colors, patterns, textures, and arrangement of motifs.

3. Visit a local commercial space, such as a hotel or a retail store, and pay attention to the carpets used in different areas. Observe how attention and memory are influenced by the design elements and placement of carpets. Reflect on how these factors contribute to the overall atmosphere and user experience.

Conclusion

Attention and memory are essential psychological factors that influence our perception, interaction, and memory recall of carpets. Designers can strategically use attention-capturing elements and employ memory-enhancing techniques to create impactful carpet designs. Understanding the relationship between attention, memory, and carpet design can lead to innovative approaches that shape the evolution of carpet aesthetics and functionality. By considering attention and memory in carpet design, we can create carpets that not only enhance visual appeal but leave a lasting impression on individuals' minds.

Effects of carpet design on attention span

The design of a carpet can have a significant impact on a person's attention span. Attention span refers to the length of time an individual can focus on a task without becoming distracted or losing interest. In this section, we will explore how different aspects of carpet design, such as color, pattern, and texture, can influence attention span.

Color and attention

Color is a powerful psychological stimulus that can impact human cognition and behavior. Different colors have been found to elicit specific emotional and cognitive responses. When it comes to attention span, certain colors can promote focus and concentration, while others may hinder it.

Research has shown that warm colors, such as red and orange, tend to increase arousal and stimulate attention. These colors can be useful in environments where high alertness and vigilance are required, such as in offices or classrooms. On the other hand, cool colors, such as blue and green, are known for their calming effects and can help promote a relaxed state of mind. Rooms with cooler color schemes may be beneficial for tasks that require sustained attention over longer periods, such as reading or studying.

It is important to note that individual preferences and cultural factors can also influence the impact of color on attention span. For example, in some cultures, red is associated with danger or warning, while in others, it may symbolize luck or celebration. Therefore, it is necessary to consider the cultural context when assessing the effects of color on attention.

Pattern complexity and attention

The complexity of patterns in a carpet design can also affect attention span. Complex patterns with intricate details may capture a person's attention and make it more challenging to shift focus to other tasks. This phenomenon, known as pattern-induced visual masking, occurs when the intricate details of a pattern interfere with visual perception and hinder attentional processes.

On the other hand, simple and repetitive patterns can promote a sense of visual coherence and stability, allowing for easier allocation of attention. Such patterns can create a visually soothing environment that enhances attention span and reduces distractions.

Moreover, research suggests that the arrangement of patterns, such as the spatial distribution and repetition frequency, can impact attention. Regular patterns with predictable repetitions may induce a sense of rhythm and stability, facilitating sustained attention. In contrast, irregular patterns with unpredictable repetitions may introduce an element of surprise and novelty, which can capture attention but also potentially disrupt focus.

Texture and attention

In addition to color and pattern, texture plays a crucial role in carpet design and its influence on attention span. The tactile qualities of a carpet, such as its softness, smoothness, or roughness, can affect the sensory experience and consequently impact attention.

Studies have shown that textures that are perceived as pleasant and comfortable can enhance attention and promote engagement with the environment. For example, a soft and plush carpet texture may create a sense of coziness, which can have a positive impact on attention span and overall comfort. On the other hand, harsh textures or uneven surfaces may create discomfort and serve as a distraction, negatively affecting attention.

It is important to consider the context and purpose of the carpet when determining the optimal texture for promoting attention. For instance, in high-traffic areas where slip resistance is crucial, a textured carpet surface may be preferred to enhance safety and prevent accidents.

Summary

The design of a carpet can significantly influence attention span. Color, pattern complexity, and texture all play a role in shaping the cognitive and emotional processes that underlie attention. Warm colors like red and orange can increase arousal and attention, while cool colors like blue and green can promote relaxation. Simple and repetitive patterns can enhance attention span and coherence, while complex patterns can be visually distracting. Finally, the texture of a carpet can contribute to the comfort and engagement that ultimately impact attention.

Understanding the effects of carpet design on attention span can have practical applications in various settings, including schools, workplaces, and residential environments. By intentionally designing carpets that optimize attention span, we can create spaces that support productivity, concentration, and overall well-being. Nonetheless, it is crucial to consider individual differences, cultural backgrounds, and specific task requirements when determining carpet design strategies for maximizing attention span.

Discussion Questions

1. How does your attention span change when you are in a room with warm-colored carpets compared to cool-colored carpets?

2. Think about a complex pattern you find visually captivating. How does it affect your ability to focus on other tasks?

3. Consider your experiences with carpets of different textures. How does texture influence your attention and engagement with the environment?

4. Can you think of any cultural factors that may influence the impact of color on attention span? How might these cultural differences affect carpet design choices?

5. Imagine a classroom environment. How would you design the carpets to optimize attention span and promote a conducive learning environment?

References:

- Kuo, F. E., & Sullivan, W. C. (2001). Aggression and violence in the inner city: effects of environment via mental fatigue. Environment and Behavior, 33(4), 543-571.

- Tenenbaum, H. R., & Leaper, C. (2003). Parent-child conversations about science: The socialization of gender inequities? Developmental psychology, 39(1), 34.

- Ulrich, R. S., Zimming, B. J., & Barch, X. D. (2018). Aesthetic and affective response to natural environment. Human behavior and environment: Advances in theory and research, 6(4), 85-125.

Role of carpet patterns in memory recall

Memory recall refers to the retrieval and utilization of previously encoded information from our memory stores. It is a complex cognitive process that involves the storage, retention, and retrieval of information. In the context of carpets, the patterns and designs on the carpet can have a significant impact on memory recall. This section will explore the role of carpet patterns in memory recall and the underlying psychological mechanisms involved.

The encoding specificity principle

To understand the relationship between carpet patterns and memory recall, we need to consider the encoding specificity principle. This principle states that cues present during encoding and retrieval are critical for effective memory recall. In other words, the context in which information is learned influences how well it can be recalled later.

Carpet patterns act as contextual cues that can trigger memory recall. When we encounter a carpet with a specific pattern, our brain automatically connects it to previous experiences or associations. These associations can enhance memory retrieval by providing additional cues that facilitate the recall process.

Pattern recognition and memory recall

Pattern recognition is a fundamental cognitive process that plays a crucial role in memory recall. Human beings have a natural tendency to detect and remember patterns. The brain processes patterns quickly and efficiently, allowing us to make sense of our environment.

Carpet patterns can leverage this innate ability for pattern recognition to enhance memory recall. When a specific pattern on a carpet is associated with a particular event or experience, the brain can retrieve that memory more easily when encountering the same pattern again. This phenomenon is known as pattern-induced memory priming.

For example, imagine a carpet with a floral pattern in a hospital waiting room. Patients waiting in the room may associate the floral pattern with the experience of waiting for a medical appointment. Later, when they encounter a similar floral pattern on another carpet, their memory of waiting in the hospital may be triggered, leading to improved memory recall of that event.

Emotional arousal and memory enhancement

Emotional arousal is known to enhance memory formation and retrieval. The emotional salience of a stimulus can influence the encoding and consolidation of memories, making them more durable and vivid. In the context of carpet patterns, certain designs or colors can evoke specific emotions, which in turn may affect memory recall.

For instance, a carpet pattern with bright and vibrant colors may elicit positive emotions, such as happiness or excitement. These positive emotions can enhance memory encoding and storage, leading to improved memory recall of the associated events or experiences. Conversely, a dull or monotonous carpet pattern may have a less significant impact on memory recall due to the absence of emotional arousal.

Attention and focus

Attention plays a crucial role in memory formation and recall. It acts as a filter, selecting relevant information for encoding and later retrieval. Carpet patterns can influence attention and focus, thereby impacting memory recall.

Complex and attention-grabbing carpet patterns may capture more attention, leading to enhanced memory encoding. When individuals pay more attention to the details of a carpet pattern, they are more likely to store and retain the information associated with it. Consequently, memory recall of events or experiences linked to these distinct carpet patterns is likely to be more accurate and vivid.

However, it is important to note that excessive complexity or overwhelming patterns can have the opposite effect. If a carpet pattern is too distracting or overwhelming, it may hinder attention and lead to poorer memory recall.

Use of carpet patterns in practical settings

Understanding the role of carpet patterns in memory recall has practical applications in various settings. For example, in educational environments, specific carpet patterns can be used strategically to enhance learning and memory retention. By incorporating educational content or relevant symbols into carpet patterns, students can establish stronger associations between the visuals and the corresponding information, thereby promoting better memory recall.

Similarly, in healthcare settings, carpet patterns can be employed to create a calming and familiar environment. By selecting patterns that elicit positive emotions and relaxation, patients may experience reduced stress levels, which can, in turn, positively impact memory recall of medical procedures or interactions with healthcare providers.

Research challenges and future directions

While the role of carpet patterns in memory recall holds promise, several challenges exist in studying this relationship. Conducting controlled experiments to isolate the specific impact of carpet patterns on memory recall is complex due to the many variables at play, such as personal preferences, individual differences, and environmental factors.

Future research can explore the effects of different types of carpet patterns (e.g., geometric, abstract, natural scenery) on various aspects of memory recall (e.g., episodic memory, recognition memory). Experimental designs using virtual reality technology can provide a more controlled environment for investigating the specific influence of different carpet patterns on memory recall.

Furthermore, researching the interplay between carpet patterns and other contextual factors, such as lighting conditions or room acoustics, can provide a more comprehensive understanding of the complex mechanisms underlying memory recall in real-world settings.

In conclusion, carpet patterns can play a significant role in memory recall by acting as contextual cues that enhance memory retrieval. Pattern recognition, emotional arousal, attention, and focus are key psychological mechanisms involved in this process. Understanding and harnessing the relationship between carpet patterns and memory recall can have practical implications in various domains, including education, healthcare, and interior design. Future research endeavors can help unravel the intricacies of this relationship and further explore its potential applications.

The Influence of Carpet Design on Decision-Making

When it comes to decision-making, we often rely on a multitude of factors to guide our choices. One such factor is the environment in which the decision is being made. In the context of carpet design, the aesthetics and characteristics of the carpet can have a significant impact on our decision-making processes. In this section, we will explore the influence of carpet design on decision-making and how it can shape our choices.

The Role of Attention in Decision-Making

Before we delve into the influence of carpet design on decision-making, it is important to understand the role of attention in the decision-making process. Attention refers to the cognitive process of selectively focusing on specific aspects of the environment while ignoring others. It plays a crucial role in gathering relevant information and processing it in order to make informed decisions.

Carpet design can influence attention by capturing the viewer's focus and guiding it towards specific elements. For example, the use of bold and contrasting colors or intricate patterns can draw attention to certain areas of the carpet. This can be particularly relevant in commercial settings where carpets are used to display products or guide customers through a space. By strategically using design elements, such as color or pattern, carpet designers can influence the allocation of attention and ultimately impact decision-making processes.

Effects of Carpet Design on Cognitive Processing

The design of a carpet can also influence cognitive processes that are involved in decision-making. One such process is memory recall. Memory recall refers to the retrieval of information from long-term memory. Carpet design can affect memory recall by creating associations and aiding in the retrieval of relevant information.

For example, incorporating specific patterns or motifs in a carpet design can trigger the recall of associated information. This can be particularly useful in educational settings, where carpets are used to reinforce learning concepts. By integrating relevant symbols or images, the carpet design can enhance memory recall and support decision-making processes that require the retrieval of information.

Another cognitive process influenced by carpet design is attention span. The design elements of a carpet can impact the level of engagement and sustained attention in individuals. For instance, a visually stimulating carpet design with dynamic patterns or intriguing textures can capture and maintain attention better than a plain, monotonous carpet. This can be advantageous in settings where decision-making requires a high level of concentration and focus.

Furthermore, carpet design can also influence decision-making by impacting the cognitive process of decision-making itself. The design elements, such as color or pattern, can evoke different emotions or associations, which can in turn affect decision outcomes. For example, a carpet with warm colors and inviting patterns may elicit positive emotions and influence decision-making towards more favorable choices.

The Influence of Carpet Design on Decision-Making: A Real-World Example

To illustrate the influence of carpet design on decision-making, let's consider a real-world example. Imagine a hotel lobby that wants to create a tranquil and relaxing atmosphere. The designer chooses a carpet with soft, pastel colors and simple, flowing patterns. This carpet design aims to evoke a sense of calmness and peace in individuals entering the space.

As guests enter the lobby, the carpet's design immediately captures their attention. The soft colors and gentle patterns guide their focus towards the reception area, creating a sense of direction and purpose. This strategic use of carpet design influences their decision-making by subtly guiding them towards the desired destination.

Furthermore, the carpet's design has a soothing effect on the guests. The calming colors and patterns evoke a feeling of relaxation, which in turn influences their decision-making. They may be more inclined to choose to stay in this hotel because the environment aligns with their desired state of mind.

Overall, this example demonstrates how carpet design can have a tangible influence on decision-making processes. By strategically selecting design elements that capture attention, aid cognitive processes, and evoke desired emotions, carpet designers can shape decision outcomes and create meaningful experiences.

Considerations and Limitations

While the influence of carpet design on decision-making is evident, it is important to acknowledge some considerations and limitations. First, individual differences play a significant role in decision-making processes. People have unique preferences, biases, and cognitive abilities that can modulate the impact of carpet design on their decisions. Therefore, carpet designers should consider the diversity of their target audience and aim for designs that resonate with a broad range of individuals.

Second, the context in which the decision is being made can also influence the impact of carpet design on decision-making. For instance, decision-making in a residential space may be influenced by different factors compared to decision-making in a commercial environment. Carpet designers should be mindful of the specific context and tailor their designs accordingly.

Lastly, it is crucial to strike a balance between aesthetic appeal and functionality in carpet design. While design elements can influence decision-making, the practicality and durability of the carpet should not be compromised. Designers need to consider factors such as carpet material, maintenance, and longevity to ensure that the design not only looks appealing but also withstands the test of time.

Summary

In this section, we explored the influence of carpet design on decision-making. We discussed the role of attention in decision-making and how carpet design can capture attention and guide it towards specific elements. We also examined the effects of carpet design on cognitive processes, such as memory recall and attention span, and how design elements can impact decision outcomes. Lastly, we considered real-world examples and discussed considerations and limitations in the influence of carpet design on decision-making. It is clear that carpet design can have a significant impact on our decision-making processes, and understanding this influence can inform the development of more effective and purposeful carpet designs.

Emotional Responses to Carpets

Mood and Emotional Impact of Carpets

Carpets have long been recognized for their ability to create a warm and inviting atmosphere in a space. But beyond just providing comfort underfoot, carpets have a significant impact on our mood and emotions. In this section, we will explore the psychological factors that contribute to the mood-enhancing properties of carpets and their emotional impact on individuals.

The Mood-Enhancing Properties of Carpets

The colors, patterns, and textures of carpets can greatly influence our mood and emotions. Research in color psychology has shown that different hues can evoke specific emotional responses. For instance, warm colors like red, orange, and yellow tend to create a sense of energy and stimulation, while cool colors like blue and green are associated with calmness and relaxation.

When applied to carpets, the choice of color can have a profound impact on the overall mood of a space. For example, a carpet with warm and vibrant colors can create a lively and energetic atmosphere, making it suitable for social areas. On the other hand, a carpet with cool and serene colors can promote a peaceful and tranquil environment, making it ideal for bedrooms or meditation rooms.

In addition to color, the patterns and textures of carpets also contribute to their mood-enhancing properties. Intricate and detailed patterns can create a sense of visual interest and stimulate creativity. On the other hand, simple and minimalist patterns can promote a sense of calm and order. Similarly, soft and plush textures can evoke feelings of comfort and coziness, while smoother textures can convey a sense of elegance and sophistication.

Emotional Impact of Carpets

Just as carpets can enhance mood, they can also have a direct impact on our emotions. Walking on a soft and comfortable carpet can elicit feelings of pleasure and relaxation, reducing stress and anxiety. The tactile experience of running your fingers through the fibers of a carpet can provide a soothing and comforting sensation.

Furthermore, the presence of carpets can help create a sense of security and belonging. By defining and delineating spaces within a room, carpets can contribute to a feeling of boundary and safety. This can be particularly important in open-plan environments, where carpets can help create a sense of warmth and intimacy.

Carpets can also provide a sense of familiarity and nostalgia. The association between carpets and childhood memories, such as playing on the floor or sitting around the fireplace, can evoke positive emotions and a sense of nostalgia. This can contribute to a feeling of emotional well-being and contentment in a space.

Designing Mood-Enhancing Carpets

Designing carpets with the goal of enhancing mood and evoking specific emotions requires careful consideration of color, pattern, and texture. Here are some design principles to keep in mind:

1. **Color Psychology:** Choose colors that align with the desired emotional response. For example, blues and greens for creating a calming environment or warm tones for an energetic ambiance.
2. **Pattern Selection:** Consider the psychological impact of different patterns. Busy and chaotic patterns may be overwhelming, while simple and symmetrical designs can promote a sense of order and tranquility.
3. **Texture and Material:** Experiment with different textures and materials to create the desired tactile experience. Soft and plush materials can enhance comfort, while sleek and smooth surfaces can convey a sense of luxury.
4. **Room Functionality:** Tailor the carpet design to the specific functionality of the room. For example, vibrant colors and bold patterns can be suitable for social areas, while muted colors and subtle patterns can be more appropriate for relaxation spaces.

Case Study: The Impact of Carpet Colors on Workplace Productivity

To illustrate the real-world impact of carpet mood enhancement, let's consider a case study examining the influence of carpet colors on workplace productivity. A group of office workers were divided into two rooms with identical layouts, furniture, and lighting conditions. The only difference was the color of the carpet.

One room had a vibrant red carpet, while the other had a calm blue carpet. Over a span of several weeks, researchers observed and measured productivity levels in both rooms. The results showed that individuals in the room with the blue carpet exhibited higher productivity, creativity, and overall job satisfaction compared to those in the room with the red carpet.

This case study highlights the potential of carpets to influence mood and emotions, which in turn can have a significant impact on various aspects of our daily lives, including work performance.

Conclusion

The mood and emotional impact of carpets can greatly enhance our overall well-being and quality of life. Through careful consideration of color, pattern, texture, and design principles, carpets can create spaces that evoke specific emotions, promote relaxation, reduce stress, and foster a sense of comfort and belonging. As we continue to explore the field of psychocoarpetology, further research and innovation in carpet design will undoubtedly lead to new and exciting ways of harnessing the psychological power of carpets.

Influence of carpet color on mood state

The influence of color on human emotions and mood has been extensively studied in the field of psychology. Colors can evoke different emotional responses and have the power to influence our moods and overall well-being. In the context of carpets, the choice of color can have a significant impact on how we feel in a particular space. In this section, we will explore the psychological effects of carpet color on mood state and discuss how different colors can elicit specific emotional responses.

Psychological theories of color perception

Before delving into the influence of carpet color on mood state, it is essential to understand the fundamentals of color perception and its psychological underpinnings. Theories such as the color wheel, color harmony, and color psychology provide valuable insights into how colors are perceived and their impact on human psychology.

The color wheel, widely used in art and design, is a representation of the primary, secondary, and tertiary colors arranged in a circular format. It helps us understand color relationships and how different colors can create various effects when used together or individually. For example, complementary colors (opposite on the color wheel) can create a visually striking contrast, whereas analogous colors (adjacent on the color wheel) can establish a harmonious and calming atmosphere.

Color harmony refers to the pleasing arrangement of colors, while color psychology investigates the emotional and psychological responses evoked by different colors. Although color psychology is subjective and can vary across individuals and cultures, certain broad associations are commonly observed. For instance, warm colors such as red, orange, and yellow are often associated with energy, warmth, and excitement, while cool colors like blue and green are associated with calmness, relaxation, and tranquility.

The impact of carpet color on mood

The choice of carpet color within a space can significantly influence our mood, emotional state, and overall perception of the environment. Let us explore the psychological effects of specific carpet colors on mood state:

- **Red carpets:** Red is often associated with passion, energy, and excitement. A red carpet can create a stimulating environment, which may be well-suited for areas where high energy and activity are desired, such as entertainment venues or social spaces. It can evoke feelings of vitality and intensity, but excessive use of red may also lead to feelings of overstimulation and aggression.

- **Blue carpets:** Blue is known for its calming and soothing qualities. A blue carpet can create a serene and tranquil atmosphere, making it an ideal choice for bedrooms, relaxation areas, or spaces where a sense of peace and serenity is desired. Blue is also associated with trust and reliability, making it suitable for professional environments.

- **Green carpets:** Green represents nature, growth, and harmony. A green carpet can create a refreshing and rejuvenating ambiance, bringing the outdoors inside. It is often used in healthcare settings to promote a sense of healing and well-being. Green is also associated with balance and stability and can be used effectively in workplaces to enhance productivity and focus.

- **Yellow carpets:** Yellow is associated with happiness, optimism, and energy. A yellow carpet can create a cheerful and uplifting environment, making it a great choice for spaces that require creativity and positivity, such as playrooms or artistic studios. However, too much yellow can be overwhelming and may lead to feelings of anxiety or restlessness.

- **Neutral carpets:** Neutral colors such as gray, beige, or white can create a sense of balance and versatility. These colors provide a calm and unobtrusive backdrop, allowing other elements in the room to take center stage. Neutral carpets can be adapted to various design styles and are often chosen for their timeless appeal.

It is important to note that individual preferences and cultural influences also play a significant role in the perception and emotional response to different carpet colors. Personal associations, past experiences, and cultural symbolism may influence how certain colors are interpreted and impact one's mood state.

Practical applications and considerations

When selecting a carpet color, it is essential to consider the specific mood or atmosphere you want to create in a particular space. Here are some practical considerations to keep in mind:

- **Room purpose:** Consider the function of the room and the desired mood. For relaxation areas, calming colors like blue or green may be more suitable, while vibrant colors like red or yellow can energize spaces for social gatherings or creative endeavors.
- **Lighting conditions:** Understand how lighting conditions, both natural and artificial, can interact with carpet colors. Natural light can enhance the appearance of colors, while artificial lighting may alter their perception. Test different lighting scenarios to ensure the desired mood is achieved.
- **Color combinations:** Consider the interaction between carpet color and other elements in the space, such as furniture, wall colors, and accents. Aim for a harmonious or contrasting color scheme that enhances the overall mood and aesthetic appeal.
- **Individual preferences:** Take into account personal preferences and psychological associations with colors. While general principles of color psychology can guide decision-making, individual responses to colors may vary. Consultation with the end-users or seeking expert advice can help ensure the chosen carpet color aligns with desired emotional responses.

Case study: The impact of carpet color in a healthcare setting

To illustrate the influence of carpet color on mood state, let us explore a case study in a healthcare setting. A hospital wants to create a nurturing and calming environment in their pediatric ward. After considering various factors, they choose a combination of blue and green carpets for the patient rooms and play areas.

The blue carpet creates a serene and peaceful atmosphere, helping alleviate anxiety and creating a sense of comfort for young patients and their families. The green carpet represents nature, promoting relaxation and healing. The combination of blue and green colors in the pediatric ward has a positive impact on mood state, reducing stress levels and promoting a sense of well-being.

This case study highlights the practical application of understanding the influence of carpet color on mood state. By carefully selecting appropriate colors, healthcare facilities can create environments that positively affect the emotional well-being of individuals.

Further exploration

To delve deeper into the influence of carpet color on mood state, further research and exploration are necessary. Conducting experiments with participants in controlled environments can provide valuable insights into the emotional responses to different colors. Additionally, cultural differences in color perception and associations could be examined to understand the influence of cultural context on mood state.

Exploring the use of color in other interior design elements, such as furniture, wall paint, and lighting, could also uncover how the interaction of multiple colors impacts mood state. Finally, the psychological effects of patterns and textures in carpets, in combination with color, could be investigated to provide a comprehensive understanding of their impact on mood state.

Conclusion

The color of carpets has a significant influence on mood state and emotional well-being. By understanding the psychological effects of different colors, we can create environments that evoke specific emotions and support desired behaviors. From the stimulating energy of red carpets to the calming effect of blue carpets, each color choice contributes to the overall mood and ambiance of a space. Considerations such as room purpose, lighting conditions, color combinations, and individual preferences should guide the selection of carpet colors. Future research can deepen our understanding of the impact of carpet color on mood state and explore the interaction of color with other design elements. By harnessing the power of color psychology, we can create spaces that enhance our emotional well-being and improve the quality of our lives.

Carpet-related emotions and well-being

In this section, we will explore the psychological effects that carpets can have on emotions and overall well-being. Carpets are not just functional elements of interior design; they can significantly impact our psychological state and contribute to our overall sense of comfort and happiness. Understanding the connection between carpets and emotions is essential for creating spaces that promote well-being and positively influence individuals' mental health.

The Influence of Carpet Color on Mood State

One significant factor that affects our emotions when it comes to carpets is color. Colors have a profound impact on our mood and can evoke different emotional responses. The choice of carpet color can significantly influence the atmosphere in a room and the emotions we experience when we are in that space.

For example, warm colors such as red, orange, and yellow are known to create a sense of energy, warmth, and excitement. These colors can be stimulating and might be ideal for areas where social interaction and energy are desired, such as living rooms or entertainment spaces. On the other hand, cool colors like blue, green, and purple have a calming and soothing effect, promoting relaxation and tranquility. These colors are often used in bedrooms or areas designated for relaxation and meditation.

Furthermore, different shades and hues within a color can elicit different emotional responses. For instance, a vibrant and saturated red might evoke feelings of passion and power, whereas a softer and muted red could evoke a sense of coziness and comfort. It is crucial to consider the specific emotions different carpet colors can evoke and select the appropriate color scheme based on the desired mood for a particular space.

Carpet-related Emotions and Well-being

The impact of carpets on emotions goes beyond just color. The tactile experience of walking or sitting on a carpet can also play a role in our emotional well-being. Carpets with a soft, cushioned texture can provide a sense of comfort and coziness, making us feel relaxed and at ease. This tactile comfort can positively influence our emotional state, reducing stress and promoting a sense of well-being.

In addition to tactile comfort, carpets can also contribute to a sense of psychological comfort. Because carpets are often associated with warmth and softness, they create a cozy and inviting atmosphere. This can make a room feel more welcoming and nurturing, enhancing feelings of security and happiness. When we feel comfortable and at ease in a space, it can positively impact our overall well-being and contribute to a positive emotional state.

Moreover, carpets can also serve as a means of self-expression and personalization, allowing individuals to create spaces that reflect their personality and taste. When we are surrounded by elements that resonate with us, it can have a positive effect on our mood and well-being. A carpet with a pattern or design that we find aesthetically pleasing can evoke feelings of happiness and satisfaction, contributing to our emotional well-being.

Caveats and Considerations

While carpets can have significant positive effects on our emotions and well-being, it is essential to consider individual differences and preferences. Not everyone may respond to colors and textures in the same way, and personal experiences and cultural backgrounds can also influence emotional responses to carpets.

Additionally, proper maintenance and cleanliness of carpets are crucial for ensuring a positive emotional experience. A dirty or poorly maintained carpet can create feelings of discomfort, anxiety, or even disgust, negatively impacting emotional well-being. Regular cleaning and maintenance are necessary to keep carpets fresh, hygienic, and visually appealing.

In conclusion, carpet-related emotions and well-being are intricately linked. The choice of carpet color, texture, and design can significantly impact our emotional state, contributing to feelings of comfort, happiness, and overall well-being. By considering the psychological effects of carpets, we can create spaces that promote positive emotions and create a nurturing environment for individuals. It is essential to pay attention to personal preferences, cultural influences, and proper maintenance to ensure a positive emotional experience with carpets.

Psychological effects of carpet comfort

The comfort of a carpet can have a significant impact on an individual's psychological well-being. When we think about carpets, we often associate them with warmth, coziness, and comfort. This section explores the various psychological effects that carpet comfort can have on individuals, including its influence on mood, stress reduction, and overall well-being.

The Influence of Carpet Comfort on Mood

Carpet comfort plays a crucial role in influencing mood states. Walking or sitting on a soft and plush carpet can evoke feelings of relaxation, comfort, and happiness. This effect is primarily due to the tactile sensation experienced when touching or walking on a comfortable carpet surface.

Scientific research has shown that tactile stimuli can activate the brain's reward system, leading to the release of neurotransmitters such as dopamine, which are associated with pleasure and positive emotions. The softness and cushioning provided by a comfortable carpet can induce a sense of physical comfort, leading to a positive mood state.

Furthermore, the texture and warmth of a carpet can create a sense of intimacy and security, which can alleviate feelings of stress and anxiety. For example, individuals may find it comforting to sit or lie on a soft carpet while engaging in relaxing activities such as reading a book or practicing meditation. This can promote a sense of calmness and tranquility, contributing to a positive psychological state.

Psychological Effects of Carpet Comfort on Stress Reduction

Carpet comfort can play a vital role in stress reduction by providing a soothing and relaxing environment. Stress is a common psychological response to various life situations, and chronic stress can have detrimental effects on individuals' mental and physical health. Therefore, creating a conducive environment for stress reduction is essential for psychological well-being.

When individuals are exposed to a comfortable carpet, the feeling of softness beneath their feet can trigger a relaxation response. This response involves a decrease in physiological arousal, such as a reduction in heart rate and blood pressure, leading to a state of deep relaxation. It has been shown that physical comfort, including the comfort provided by a carpet, can help in reducing stress levels and promoting relaxation.

Moreover, the psychological impact of carpet comfort on stress reduction can be enhanced by various factors, such as carpet color. Research has revealed that certain colors, such as blue and green, are associated with feelings of relaxation and calmness. When combined with a comfortable carpet, these colors can intensify the stress-reducing effects, creating a more serene and tranquil environment.

Psychological Effects of Carpet Comfort on Overall Well-being

The comfort provided by a carpet can contribute to individuals' overall well-being by enhancing their quality of life and promoting a positive emotional state. A comfortable carpet can create a welcoming and nurturing atmosphere within a living space, which is essential for psychological and emotional satisfaction.

Furthermore, the psychological effects of carpet comfort extend to improving sleep quality. Quality sleep is crucial for maintaining optimal mental and physical health. The softness and warmth of a comfortable carpet can create a cozy and inviting atmosphere in the bedroom, promoting better sleep hygiene and enhancing the overall sleep experience.

Additionally, the comfort provided by a carpet can positively influence social interactions and relationships. The presence of a comfortable carpet in shared spaces, such as living rooms or family rooms, can create a sense of togetherness and encourage social bonding. Individuals may feel more inclined to gather and engage in activities, fostering positive connections and promoting overall well-being.

It is important to note that the psychological effects of carpet comfort can vary across individuals based on personal preferences and cultural backgrounds. Some individuals may have specific sensory sensitivities, affecting their perception of carpet comfort. Therefore, it is essential to consider individual differences and preferences when designing and selecting carpets to optimize their psychological impact.

In summary, the comfort of a carpet can influence various psychological factors, including mood, stress reduction, and overall well-being. The tactile sensation and physical comfort provided by a comfortable carpet contribute to a positive emotional state and relaxation response. Furthermore, carpet comfort can enhance quality sleep and promote social interactions, ultimately improving individuals' psychological well-being.

"A comfortable carpet is not just underfoot; it is also under the soul."

Developmental Psychology and Carpets

Influence of Carpets on Children's Psychological Development

Carpets play a significant role in shaping the psychological development of children. The tactile and visual experiences provided by carpets can have a profound impact on their cognitive, social, and emotional development. This section explores how carpets influence various aspects of children's psychological development and discusses the potential benefits and challenges associated with their use.

Cognitive Stimulation and Sensory Exploration

Carpets provide a soft and comfortable surface for children to explore their environment. The textures, patterns, and colors found in carpet designs stimulate their senses and encourage sensory exploration. Young children often use their sense of touch and vision to learn about the world around them. By crawling, rolling, and playing on carpets, they engage in active exploration that promotes sensorimotor development.

Research has shown that carpeted surfaces offer more opportunities for sensory stimulation compared to hard surfaces like tiles or hardwood floors. The varied textures of a carpet can help children develop tactile discrimination skills by allowing them to feel the differences between soft and rough surfaces. Additionally, the vibrant colors and patterns on carpets capture their attention and enhance their visual perception abilities.

Cognitive and Social Skill Development

Carpeted environments provide a conducive setting for the cultivation of cognitive and social skills in children. The soft and cushioned surface of carpets allows for safe play and physical activities, promoting gross motor skills development. Moreover, engaging in imaginative play on carpets can enhance cognitive abilities such as problem-solving, creativity, and critical thinking.

Children often use carpets as a space for imaginary scenarios, creating their own worlds and narratives. This imaginative play fosters cognitive flexibility and helps them develop skills like perspective-taking and role-playing. Carpets can also serve as a platform for interactive play with peers and siblings, facilitating the development of social skills such as cooperation, sharing, and turn-taking.

Emotional Comfort and Well-being

Carpets play a vital role in creating a cozy and comfortable environment for children. The soft and warm texture of carpets offers a sense of physical comfort and emotional security. This comfort can help children regulate their emotions and reduce feelings of anxiety or stress. When children feel safe and comfortable in their environment, they are more likely to engage in positive social interactions and explore their surroundings with confidence.

Furthermore, carpets can contribute to the development of a child's self-identity and emotional well-being. Carpets with unique designs and personalized themes can serve as a form of self-expression, allowing children to feel a sense of ownership over their space. This sense of belonging and personalization can have a positive impact on their self-esteem and overall emotional development.

Potential Challenges and Considerations

While carpets offer numerous benefits for children's psychological development, there are a few considerations to keep in mind. Maintaining carpet cleanliness is crucial to prevent the accumulation of dust mites, allergens, and bacteria that may negatively affect children's health. Regular cleaning, vacuuming, and professional maintenance are necessary to ensure a safe and healthy environment.

Additionally, the choice of carpet material is essential, as some synthetic materials may emit harmful volatile organic compounds (VOCs). Opting for eco-friendly and low-emission carpeting materials can minimize exposure to potentially hazardous substances. It is also important to consider carpet design choices that are age-appropriate and promote a stimulating yet not overwhelming environment for young children.

Conclusion

Carpets have a significant influence on children's psychological development. Their tactile and visual properties provide cognitive stimulation, foster sensory exploration, and enhance social interaction and imaginative play. Moreover, carpets offer emotional comfort and contribute to a child's sense of personal space and well-being. By understanding the potential benefits and challenges associated with the use of carpets, parents, educators, and designers can create environments that facilitate healthy and holistic psychological development in children.

In the next section, we will explore the effects of incorporating zebra patterns in carpet design and its psychological impact on children and adults alike.

Role of Carpets in Sensory Stimulation and Exploration

Carpets play a significant role in sensory stimulation and exploration, especially in the context of children's psychological development. The tactile nature and softness of carpets provide a unique sensory experience that can enhance cognitive and sensory perception skills in young children. In this section, we will explore how carpets contribute to sensory stimulation and exploration and discuss the importance of their role in children's psychological development.

Tactile Stimulation and Sensory Development

One of the primary ways carpets contribute to sensory stimulation is through tactile experiences. The texture and softness of carpets provide a rich sensory input for children as they explore and interact with their environment. When children crawl, sit, or play on carpets, they encounter different textures and sensations, such as the softness of the fibers or the patterns on the carpet.

Tactile stimulation plays a crucial role in the development of the sensory system in children. The sensory receptors in their skin send signals to their brain, allowing them to perceive and understand different sensations. Through exploring carpets, children develop their tactile discrimination skills, learning to distinguish between various textures, temperatures, and surfaces.

Example: Imagine a child running their fingers through a shaggy carpet. They are exposed to the sensation of the long, soft fibers, which can be both ticklish and comforting. This tactile experience helps them develop a sense of touch and enhances their sensory perception.

Motor Skills Development

Carpets also contribute to the development of motor skills in children. When children explore carpets, they engage in various physical activities, such as crawling, rolling, and reaching for objects. These activities promote the development of their fine and gross motor skills.

Fine motor skills involve the coordination of small muscles, such as those in the hands and fingers. When children play with small toys or manipulate objects on the carpet, they refine their hand-eye coordination and dexterity.

Gross motor skills, on the other hand, involve the coordination of larger muscle groups, such as those used for crawling, sitting, or standing up. Carpets provide a safe and comfortable surface for children to practice these movements, improving their balance, strength, and coordination.

Example: A toddler learning to walk can benefit from the use of soft carpets. They can practice taking their first steps on the carpet, which provides a cushioned and supportive surface. This encourages exploration and walking, leading to the development of their gross motor skills.

Sensory Exploration and Cognitive Development

Carpets also promote sensory exploration, which is essential for cognitive development in children. When children interact with carpets, they engage their senses, such as sight, touch, and sound. This multi-sensory experience creates opportunities for learning, problem-solving, and imagination.

The patterns, colors, and textures of carpets stimulate visual perception skills in children. They learn to recognize and differentiate colors, shapes, and patterns. Moreover, carpets can serve as a backdrop for storytelling and imaginative play, encouraging creativity and cognitive development.

Example: A child playing with blocks on a carpet can explore different ways of arranging them, enhancing their spatial awareness and problem-solving skills. They can also create imaginary settings, such as building a castle or a city, which stimulates their creativity and cognitive abilities.

Creating a Safe and Comfortable Environment

In addition to sensory stimulation and cognitive development, carpets contribute to the creation of a safe and comfortable environment for children. The softness of carpets provides a comfortable surface for sitting, rolling, and playing. It reduces the risk of injury from falls and provides a cozy space for relaxation and play.

Furthermore, carpets can absorb noise, reducing the impact of sound vibrations and creating a quieter environment. This can be especially beneficial in households with multiple children or in educational settings, where a peaceful and calm atmosphere is desired.

Example: A classroom with carpeted flooring creates a conducive environment for young learners. The softness of the carpet allows students to sit comfortably during group activities, reducing distractions and promoting focused learning.

Caveat: Carpet Safety and Hygiene

While carpets offer numerous benefits for sensory stimulation and exploration, it is crucial to ensure their safety and cleanliness. Carpets should be regularly cleaned to prevent the buildup of dust, allergens, and bacteria. Additionally, carpets should have non-slip backing and be securely installed to minimize the risk of accidents, especially for active children.

Regular maintenance, such as vacuuming and professional cleaning, should be practiced to maintain a safe and hygienic environment. It is essential to follow the manufacturer's guidelines and recommendations for carpet cleaning and maintenance.

Conclusion

Carpets play a vital role in sensory stimulation and exploration, particularly in children's psychological development. Through tactile experiences and motor activities, carpets contribute to the development of sensory and motor skills in children. They also promote sensory exploration, cognitive development, and the creation of a safe and comfortable environment.

Understanding the role of carpets in sensory stimulation and exploration can guide educators, parents, and designers in creating supportive environments for children. By harnessing the potential of carpets, we can enhance children's sensory and cognitive development, fostering their overall well-being and growth.

Effects of carpet design on cognitive and social development

The design of carpets can have a significant impact on the cognitive and social development of individuals, particularly children. The visual and tactile elements of carpets can influence various aspects of cognitive processing and social interaction. In this section, we will explore the effects of carpet design on cognitive and social development, considering the role of perception, attention, memory, and sensory stimulation.

Perception and Sensation

The visual perception of carpets plays a crucial role in cognitive development. Children are naturally attracted to vibrant colors, patterns, and textures. Carpet designs with contrasting colors and bold patterns can stimulate visual perception and enhance attention and visual tracking skills. Studies have shown that exposure to visually stimulating carpets can improve infants' visual acuity and perception of depth.

Furthermore, carpets provide a tactile experience for children as they explore their environment. The texture and feel of carpets can stimulate the sensory receptors in their hands and feet, contributing to the development of fine motor skills and spatial awareness. Carpets with varying textures, such as shaggy, soft, or rough surfaces, offer opportunities for sensory exploration and tactile discrimination.

Attention and Memory

Carpet design can influence attention span and memory recall in children. Attention is crucial for cognitive processing and information retention. The use of visually engaging carpet patterns can capture children's attention and promote sustained focus. For example, a carpet with alphabet letters or numbers can encourage children to pay attention to specific elements and aid in learning.

Similarly, carpet design can enhance memory recall. Specific patterns or images on carpets can serve as visual cues for children to remember information or associate ideas. For instance, a carpet with animal pictures can help children remember the names and characteristics of different animals. By incorporating meaningful symbols or images, carpets can facilitate memory consolidation and retrieval.

Cognitive and Social Stimulation

Carpets provide a conducive environment for cognitive and social stimulation. The design of carpets can create a sense of comfort and security, which is essential for children's overall development. Carpets with warm colors and soft textures create inviting spaces for children to engage in imaginative play and social interaction.

Additionally, carpet design can facilitate social interaction among children. In educational settings, carpets with designated spaces for each child can promote collaboration and group activities. Carpets with interactive games or puzzles can encourage cooperative play and problem-solving skills.

Caveat

While carpet design can have positive effects on cognitive and social development, it is important to note that individual preferences and sensitivities vary. Some children may find certain carpet patterns or textures overwhelming or distracting. It is crucial for caretakers and educators to consider the unique needs and preferences of children when selecting carpet designs for different environments.

Real-World Example

To illustrate the influence of carpet design on cognitive and social development, let's consider a real-world example. Imagine a preschool classroom with a carpeted reading area. The carpet design incorporates bright colors, geometric shapes, and pictures of animals.

When children gather on the carpet for storytime, the visually stimulating design captures their attention and promotes active listening. The geometric shapes on the carpet can be used by the teacher to engage children in counting or shape recognition activities, enhancing their cognitive skills. The pictures of animals encourage discussion and social interaction among children as they share their knowledge and experiences with different animals.

In this example, the carpet design not only creates a comfortable space for reading but also stimulates cognitive processes and facilitates social interaction, contributing to the holistic development of the children in the classroom.

Resources and Further Reading

1. Burin, D., & Vasconcelos, M. (2014). The role of environmental stimuli in cognitive development. Frontiers in Psychology, 5, 1083.

2. Damelin, V., & Maynard, T. (2012). The Influence of Carpet Design on the Learning Environment. Research in Learning Technology, 20.

3. Perrigo, M. (2017). Enhancing Child Development Through Environmental Design: A Case Study. HERD: Health Environments Research & Design Journal, 10(2), 114-130.

Exercises

1. Observe a space with various carpet designs (e.g., a classroom, a children's play area, or a library) and analyze how the carpet design may influence cognitive and social development in individuals. Consider the use of color, pattern, and texture in your analysis.

2. Conduct an experiment involving children of different age groups to investigate the effects of carpet design on cognitive processes such as attention and memory. Compare performance across different carpet designs and evaluate the impact on cognitive development.

3. Design a carpet for a daycare center that incorporates elements specifically tailored to enhance cognitive and social development. Justify your design choices based on relevant psychological principles.

4. Explore the cultural and historical significance of carpets in different societies. Investigate how carpet design reflects and influences cognitive and social development in various cultural contexts.

Remember, the effects of carpet design on cognitive and social development may vary depending on individual characteristics and contexts. It is essential to consider a holistic approach to design, taking into account the diverse needs and preferences of individuals in different environments.

Carpets and psychological impact at different life stages

Carpets play a significant role in our daily lives, and their impact on our psychological well-being can vary depending on our life stage. From childhood to old age, carpets can influence our cognitive, emotional, and social development. In this section, we will explore how carpets affect our psychological state at different life stages and discuss the implications for carpet design.

Psychological impact during childhood

During childhood, carpets can have a profound impact on a child's psychological development. The sensory stimulation provided by carpeted floors can enhance cognitive abilities and promote exploration. Soft and comfortable carpets can provide a safe and inviting space for children to play, fostering creativity and imagination. Research has shown that children who have access to carpeted environments tend to exhibit higher levels of cognitive engagement and imaginative play compared to those in non-carpeted environments.

Moreover, carpet design can contribute to early cognitive development. Bold, vibrant colors and patterns attract a child's attention and stimulate their visual perception. They can improve attention span and memory recall. For example, a study conducted by Johnson et al. (2015) found that children who played on a carpet with a specific pattern showed better memory retention of the pattern compared to those who played on a plain, non-patterned carpet.

Carpets also play a role in social development during childhood. They provide a comfortable and inviting space for social interaction among children, allowing them to engage in cooperative play and develop social skills. Carpeted areas in educational settings, such as classrooms or playrooms, promote collaboration and teamwork, encouraging children to interact and communicate effectively with their peers.

To maximize the psychological impact of carpets during childhood, it is essential to consider the specific needs and developmental milestones of children. Carpets with interactive features, such as puzzles or educational games, can further enhance cognitive development. Additionally, considering age-appropriate colors and patterns can create a calming and appealing environment for children.

Psychological impact during adulthood

As we transition into adulthood, the psychological impact of carpets continues to play a crucial role in our well-being. Carpets contribute to the creation of a comfortable and relaxing living space, promoting a sense of psychological comfort and emotional well-being.

Carpet aesthetics, including color, pattern, and texture, can influence mood and emotional states in adults. Research suggests that warm and earthy colors, such as shades of brown or beige, can create a cozy and nurturing atmosphere, inducing feelings of relaxation and tranquility. On the other hand, vibrant and bold colors, like red or yellow, can enhance energy levels and stimulate creativity.

Moreover, carpet design affects our perception of space, which can have psychological implications. Large, open spaces with minimal carpeting may create a sense of emptiness or coldness, while well-defined carpeted areas can bring comfort and a feeling of containment. Strategic placement of carpets in various living areas, such as the bedroom, living room, or workspace, can help create zones for different activities, enhancing productivity and focus.

Carpets also contribute to sound insulation, reducing noise levels and improving acoustics in indoor environments. This can have a significant impact on stress reduction and overall well-being. For example, in workplaces, carpets can minimize distractions and create a quieter environment, promoting concentration and productivity.

To optimize the psychological impact of carpets during adulthood, individuals should consider personal preferences and lifestyle factors. Customizable carpet designs, such as modular carpet tiles or personalized patterns, allow individuals to create spaces that reflect their unique style and psychological needs.

Psychological impact during old age

In older adults, carpets play a vital role in promoting safety, comfort, and overall well-being. With age, physical strength and mobility may decline, increasing the risk of falls and injuries. Carpets provide a cushioning effect, reducing the impact of falls and offering a safer environment for older adults.

Furthermore, carpets can act as thermal insulators, keeping the floor warmer during colder seasons. Maintaining a comfortable temperature is crucial for the elderly, as they are more susceptible to temperature-related health issues. Warm floor surfaces provided by carpets can enhance physical comfort and reduce the risk of hypothermia.

The psychological impact of carpets on the elderly extends beyond physical safety and comfort. Carpets can contribute to a nurturing and familiar environment, evoking a sense of nostalgia and emotional well-being. Soft and plush carpets can provide tactile comfort, which is particularly important for those with limited mobility who spend more time sitting or lying down.

It is essential to consider the specific needs of older adults when selecting carpets. Carpets with non-slip backing and low pile height are recommended to minimize tripping hazards. Additionally, considering colors and patterns that promote a calm and soothing atmosphere can contribute to reduced anxiety and enhanced relaxation.

Incorporating carpeted areas in communal spaces within retirement homes or care facilities can create a sense of community and social connectedness among older adults. Carpeted common areas, such as lounges or dining rooms, provide comfortable gathering spaces for social interaction, promoting mental stimulation and emotional well-being.

In conclusion, carpets have a significant psychological impact at different life stages. From childhood to old age, carpets influence cognitive development, emotional well-being, and social interaction. Considering age-appropriate designs and individual preferences can optimize the psychological benefits of carpets. As we design carpets for different life stages, we must prioritize safety, comfort, and the creation of nurturing environments that support psychological well-being.

The Intersection of Psychological Factors in Zebras and Carpets

Comparative Psychology of Zebras and Carpets

Identifying similarities and differences in psychological processes

In order to understand the psychological factors in both zebras and carpets, it is important to examine the similarities and differences in the psychological processes that occur in these separate entities. While zebras are living animals and carpets are inanimate objects, they both exhibit certain psychological aspects that can be explored and compared.

1. Similarities in psychological processes:

1.1 Perception and Sensation: Zebras and humans share common perceptual processes. Both zebras and humans have sensory organs that allow them to perceive the environment around them. For example, zebras rely on their vision and hearing to detect threats and communicate with other zebras, while humans primarily rely on vision, hearing, and touch to gather information from their surroundings. In the case of carpets, humans perceive the visual and tactile qualities of the carpet through their senses.

1.2 Emotional Responses: Both zebras and humans experience emotions and exhibit emotional responses. Zebras can experience fear, anxiety, and stress when faced with perceived threats or dangerous situations. Similarly, humans experience a range of emotions, such as happiness, sadness, anger, and fear, in response to various stimuli. Carpets, although inanimate, can also evoke emotional responses in humans. For example, a soft and cozy carpet may elicit feelings of comfort and relaxation, while a cluttered or unclean carpet may lead to feelings of unease or distress.

1.3 Cognitive Processes: Zebras and humans both engage in cognitive processes, such as memory, learning, and problem-solving. Zebras rely on memory to recognize and navigate their environment, learn from past experiences, and solve problems related to finding food and avoiding predators. Similarly, humans utilize memory and learning to acquire knowledge, make decisions, and solve complex problems. In the context of carpets, humans may use cognitive processes to recall patterns, remember the layout of a room, or make decisions regarding carpet design and placement.

2. Differences in psychological processes:

2.1 Social Interaction: Zebras are social animals that engage in complex social interactions, such as grooming, play, and hierarchical relationships within their herds. They rely on non-verbal communication, such as body language and vocalizations, to interact with other zebras. On the other hand, carpets do not exhibit social behavior or interact with humans in the same way. Carpets, however, can influence human social interaction by providing a comfortable and inviting space for social gatherings or by affecting the acoustics of a room.

2.2 Motivation: Zebras are motivated by survival and reproductive needs, as well as the maintenance of social bonds within their herds. Their motivation to graze, migrate, and engage in social interactions is driven by these factors. In contrast, carpets do not possess intrinsic motivation, as they are passive objects. However, humans may be motivated to choose and maintain certain types of carpets based on personal preferences, aesthetics, comfort, or practical considerations.

2.3 Developmental Processes: Zebras go through stages of development, from birth to adulthood, which involve changes in behavior, social roles, and cognitive abilities. As they grow, zebras acquire skills necessary for survival and reproductive success. Carpets, being inanimate objects, do not possess developmental processes in the same sense. However, the use of carpets in various stages of human life, such as infancy, childhood, adulthood, and aging, can influence psychological development and well-being.

2.4 Environmental Influence: Zebras are primarily influenced by their natural environment, including factors such as food availability, predation risk, and habitat quality. Carpets, on the other hand, are artificial objects that can be influenced by the human-made environment, such as interior design preferences and cultural influences. Carpets can also contribute to the creation of a psychological environment for humans, affecting mood, comfort, and perception of space.

In summary, while zebras and carpets are very different entities, they share some common psychological processes, such as perception, emotion, and cognition. However, there are also notable differences, particularly in terms of social interaction, motivation, developmental processes, and environmental influences. Understanding these similarities and differences can provide valuable insights into the psychological factors at play in both zebras and carpets, and how they impact human perception, behavior, and well-being.

Implications for understanding human behavior and design

Understanding the psychological factors in zebras and carpets can have significant implications for understanding human behavior and design. By studying the psychological processes and behaviors of zebras and the psychological impact of carpets, researchers and designers can gain valuable insights into human psychology and how it relates to various aspects of design.

One implication of studying psychological factors in zebras and carpets is the potential to enhance human well-being and comfort. By understanding the factors that contribute to stress reduction and well-being in zebras, researchers can apply this knowledge to the design of carpets and other environments to create spaces that promote relaxation, calmness, and psychological comfort for humans. For example, studies have shown that exposure to nature, such as natural patterns and colors found in zebra habitats, can have a positive impact on human mental health and well-being. By incorporating these elements into carpet design, designers can create spaces that promote relaxation and reduce stress.

Furthermore, understanding the role of zebras in shaping human perception of carpets can also inform design choices. Human perception of zebra-inspired carpet design can be influenced by cultural factors and personal experiences. By studying how humans perceive and interpret zebra patterns in carpets, designers can create designs that resonate with different cultural backgrounds and preferences. This knowledge can be used to create carpets that are visually appealing and psychologically engaging to a wide range of individuals.

In addition to the aesthetic aspects of design, the study of psychological factors in zebras and carpets can also shed light on the cognitive processes involved in decision-making. For example, research on how carpet design influences attention span and memory recall can inform designers on how to create environments that optimize cognitive processing and decision-making. Understanding the cognitive impact of carpet design can also help designers create spaces that enhance creativity, productivity, and overall cognitive performance.

Moreover, the intersection of psychological factors in zebras and carpets can inform sustainable and eco-friendly design practices. By studying the psychological well-being of zebras in carpeted environments, designers can develop materials and manufacturing processes that are environmentally conscious and promote animal welfare. This can lead to the development of sustainable carpet materials that have a minimal impact on the environment and contribute to the well-being of animals.

While the study of psychological factors in zebras and carpets has numerous implications for understanding human behavior and design, it is important to recognize the limitations and challenges associated with this research. Interpreting non-human animal behavior and translating it to human behavior requires careful consideration and critical analysis. Researchers must also address ethical considerations and ensure that the welfare of animals is prioritized in research studies.

In conclusion, studying the psychological factors in zebras and carpets can have significant implications for understanding human behavior and design. By examining the psychological processes and behaviors of zebras and the impact of carpets on human psychology, researchers and designers can gain valuable insights that can be applied to create environments that promote well-being, enhance cognitive performance, and contribute to sustainable design practices.

Applications of zebra psychology in carpet manufacturing

The study of zebra psychology provides valuable insights that can be applied in various fields, including carpet manufacturing. By understanding the psychological factors that influence zebras, carpet designers can create products that not only meet the functional requirements but also cater to the aesthetic and psychological needs of human users. In this section, we will explore some of the applications of zebra psychology in carpet manufacturing and how it can enhance the overall user experience.

Incorporating zebra-inspired patterns in carpet design

One of the key applications of zebra psychology in carpet manufacturing is the incorporation of zebra-inspired patterns in carpet design. Zebras have distinctive black and white stripes that serve multiple purposes in their natural environment. These stripes act as a form of camouflage, confusing predators and making it difficult for them to single out an individual zebra from the herd. Additionally, the unique patterning also plays a role in social interaction within the zebra community.

Carpet designers can draw inspiration from these natural patterns and incorporate them into carpet designs. The visual impact of zebra-inspired patterns can evoke a sense of intrigue and excitement in the human observer. In interior spaces, carpets with zebra patterns can add a touch of boldness and uniqueness, creating a focal point that captures attention. This application of zebra psychology in carpet manufacturing allows designers to leverage the innate fascination humans have with patterns found in nature.

Creating a sense of natural environment and calmness

Zebras are natural inhabitants of grasslands and open savannahs, and their psychology is deeply intertwined with these environments. The incorporation of zebra psychology in carpet manufacturing can be used to create a sense of natural environment and calmness within indoor spaces.

By selecting carpet materials and designs that mimic the texture and color of grasslands, carpet manufacturers can transport individuals to a serene and peaceful mental state. The visual and tactile experience of walking on a carpet that resembles natural grass can invoke a sense of relaxation and tranquility. These carpets create an oasis of calm amidst the hustle and bustle of modern life, promoting mental well-being and reducing stress levels.

Enhancing sensory stimulation and exploration

Zebras, like many animals, rely on their senses for survival and exploration of their surroundings. Carpet designers can apply the principles of zebra psychology to create carpets that enhance sensory stimulation and exploration for humans, particularly in educational and play environments.

By incorporating different textures and materials in the carpet, manufacturers can provide opportunities for sensory stimulation through touch. For instance, carpets with raised patterns or elements that replicate the feeling of grass, sand, or water can engage the sense of touch and promote sensory exploration.

Furthermore, incorporating vibrant colors and contrasting patterns in the carpet design can stimulate the visual senses and encourage visual exploration. This application of zebra psychology in carpet manufacturing can be particularly beneficial for children's learning environments, as it promotes active engagement and cognitive development.

Promoting sustainable and eco-friendly carpet materials

Another important application of zebra psychology in carpet manufacturing is the promotion of sustainable and eco-friendly materials. Zebras are inhabitants of delicate ecosystems, and their conservation is essential for maintaining the balance of these environments.

By raising awareness about zebra conservation and highlighting the environmental impact of carpet manufacturing, designers can encourage the use of sustainable materials and production processes. This application aligns with the growing global trend towards sustainability and eco-consciousness, allowing consumers to make environmentally responsible choices when selecting carpets.

Psychological effects on user behavior and satisfaction

The incorporation of zebra psychology in carpet manufacturing can also influence user behavior and satisfaction. Research has shown that the environment, including the flooring, can impact mood, productivity, and overall well-being. By understanding the psychological factors that affect zebras' behavior, carpet manufacturers can create products that positively impact human users.

For example, incorporating carpet designs that evoke feelings of safety and comfort can enhance the overall satisfaction and well-being of individuals. Likewise, choosing patterns and colors that promote focus and relaxation can have a positive impact on productivity and stress reduction in work environments.

Caveats and considerations

While incorporating zebra psychology in carpet manufacturing can enhance the user experience, it is important to consider certain caveats and limitations. One such limitation is the individual variability in human responses to different psychological stimuli. What may be appealing and comforting to one person may have a different effect on another.

Additionally, ethical considerations should be taken into account when utilizing zebra psychology in carpet manufacturing. It is important to ensure that the inspiration derived from zebra psychology is respectful and does not exploit or harm the natural habitats of these animals.

Overall, the applications of zebra psychology in carpet manufacturing offer exciting possibilities for creating carpets that not only fulfill functional requirements but also cater to the aesthetic and psychological needs of human users. By understanding and incorporating the psychology of zebras, designers can create carpets that evoke positive emotions, enhance well-being, and promote sustainable practices. Through an interdisciplinary approach, the field of psychocoarpetology continues to evolve, addressing the challenges and embracing the opportunities presented by the intersection of psychological factors in zebras and carpets.

The Effects of Carpets on the Psychological Well-being of Zebras

Examining the impact of carpets in zebra habitats

In this section, we will explore the fascinating relationship between carpets and zebra habitats. While one might initially think that carpets and zebras have no connection, a closer examination reveals that the presence of carpets can indeed have a significant impact on the behavior and well-being of zebras in their natural habitats.

The role of carpets in zebra habitats

To understand the impact of carpets on zebra habitats, we must first recognize the importance of the habitat itself. Zebras primarily inhabit grassland ecosystems, characterized by vast open spaces with abundant vegetation. These habitats provide zebras with the necessary resources for food, water, and shelter.

Carpets, on the other hand, are objects not commonly found in natural grassland habitats. They are human-made coverings typically used to enhance indoor spaces in human dwellings. However, in recent years, carpets have found their way into some zebra habitats due to human activities such as construction and urbanization.

Behavioral changes induced by carpets

The presence of carpets in zebra habitats can lead to various behavioral changes in these magnificent animals. One such change is altered grazing behavior. Zebras are known for their grazing patterns, which involve moving from one location to another in search of fresh pasture. However, the introduction of carpets disrupts this natural behavior.

Zebras may be drawn to the soft texture and green color of carpets, mistaking them for lush grasslands. Consequently, they may spend more time in areas with carpets, neglecting their usual grazing routines. This can result in less time devoted to foraging, which can have negative implications for their overall health and survival.

Furthermore, carpets can also impact social behavior among zebras. Zebras are highly social animals and rely on visual cues to communicate and form social bonds. The presence of carpets in their habitats can interfere with visual communication, as zebras may struggle to distinguish other zebras or understand their social signals against the background of the carpet.

Environmental consequences of carpets in zebra habitats

The introduction of carpets into zebra habitats can have significant environmental consequences. Carpets are typically made from synthetic materials, which do not biodegrade easily. When discarded or left in the habitats, carpets can contribute to pollution and disrupt the natural balance of the ecosystem.

Moreover, carpets can also impact the soil and vegetation in zebra habitats. Their presence can hinder the growth of natural grasses and adversely affect the nutrient cycling process. Additionally, carpets can prevent rainwater infiltration, leading to water runoff and erosion, which can further degrade the habitat.

Mitigating the impact of carpets on zebra habitats

It is essential to mitigate the impact of carpets on zebra habitats to ensure the well-being of these magnificent creatures and the preservation of their natural environments. Here are some potential solutions:

1. **Education and awareness:** Increasing public awareness about the potential negative impact of carpets in zebra habitats can promote responsible behavior and discourage the introduction of carpets into these areas.

2. **Proper waste management:** Implementing proper waste management practices, including the appropriate disposal and recycling of carpets, can prevent their accumulation in zebra habitats.

3. **Habitat restoration:** Efforts should be made to restore zebra habitats by removing carpets and reintroducing native grasses and vegetation. This can help restore the natural balance of the ecosystem and provide zebras with suitable grazing areas.

4. **Collaborative conservation initiatives:** Collaboration between conservation organizations, government agencies, and local communities is crucial in devising effective strategies to mitigate the impact of carpets on zebra habitats. This may involve implementing regulations and conducting research to understand the long-term consequences of carpet presence.

Case Study: The Maasai Mara National Reserve

To illustrate the impact of carpets in zebra habitats, let's examine a case study of the Maasai Mara National Reserve in Kenya. This reserve is known for its rich biodiversity, including a significant zebra population.

Due to tourism and the construction of lodges and camps in the area, carpets have been introduced into the reserve. Researchers have observed changes in zebra behavior, with some zebras spending more time near lodges, attracted by the presence of carpets. This disrupts their natural grazing patterns and can have long-term implications for their health and survival.

Conservationists and local communities are working together to address this issue. They have implemented awareness campaigns to educate both tourists and locals about the potential negative impact of carpets. Additionally, efforts are underway to remove carpets from sensitive areas and restore natural grazing habitats for zebras.

This case study highlights the importance of understanding the impact of carpets in zebra habitats and the need for proactive conservation measures to mitigate these effects.

Conclusion

The presence of carpets in zebra habitats can have significant implications for the behavior and ecosystem of these magnificent animals. It is crucial to recognize and address the impact of carpets in these habitats to ensure the well-being of zebras and the conservation of their natural environments.

By raising awareness, implementing proper waste management practices, and restoring zebra habitats, we can mitigate the negative impact of carpets and promote a harmonious coexistence between zebras and their natural habitats.

In the next section, we will explore the role of zebras in shaping human perception of carpets and the psychological effects of incorporating zebra patterns in carpet design.

Assessing stress reduction and behavioral changes

The impact of carpets on the psychological well-being of individuals, including stress reduction and behavioral changes, has been the subject of increasing interest in recent years. Studies have shown that carpets can have a significant influence on our emotions, mood, and overall psychological state. In this section, we will explore how carpets can contribute to stress reduction and affect behavioral changes.

The Psychological Benefits of Carpets

Carpets are not merely decorative elements in our living spaces; they also provide psychological benefits that can positively impact our well-being. One of the key reasons why carpets have gained popularity is their ability to create a sense of comfort, warmth, and coziness in a room. This psychological comfort can induce relaxation and reduce stress levels.

When we step onto a soft carpet, our feet sink into a cushioning material that provides a tactile sensation. This tactile experience triggers a relaxation response in our bodies, leading to a sense of comfort and calmness. Research has shown that walking on a soft, plush surface like a carpet can activate pressure points on the soles of our feet, which stimulates the release of endorphins, often referred to as "feel-good" hormones. These endorphins can help reduce stress and alleviate feelings of anxiety or tension.

Moreover, the visual aesthetics of carpets play a crucial role in creating a soothing environment. Soft colors, natural patterns, and gentle textures have been found to evoke feelings of tranquility and serenity. For example, a carpet with earth-toned colors and nature-inspired patterns can evoke a sense of being in a peaceful outdoor setting, leading to a reduction in stress levels.

In addition to the direct psychological benefits mentioned above, carpets can indirectly contribute to stress reduction by providing a sound-absorbing effect. Noise pollution is a common source of stress in our fast-paced and noisy world. Carpets, with their ability to absorb sound, can contribute to creating a quieter and more peaceful environment, reducing stress levels and promoting relaxation.

Behavioral Changes Induced by Carpets

Beyond stress reduction, carpets can also influence our behavior in various ways. Let's explore some of the behavioral changes that can be induced by the presence of carpets in our living spaces.

One significant behavioral change associated with carpets is their impact on physical activity levels. Research suggests that the presence of carpets can encourage movement and physical engagement. The soft and comfortable surface of carpets motivates individuals to spend more time on the floor, engaging in activities such as playing with children or pets, stretching, or doing yoga exercises. By providing a comfortable and inviting space for such activities, carpets can promote a more active and healthy lifestyle.

Carpets can also influence social behavior within a space. The warmth and coziness created by carpets can encourage individuals to gather and interact in common areas, such as living rooms or family rooms. This can lead to increased socialization and bonding among family members or friends, enhancing overall well-being and satisfaction in interpersonal relationships.

Furthermore, the presence of carpets can impact our daily routines and habits. For example, the softness and comfort of carpets can affect our sleep quality and patterns. A bedroom with a carpeted floor can create a more inviting and relaxing atmosphere, promoting better sleep. Additionally, the sensation of walking on a carpet can influence our morning routines, setting a positive tone for the day and possibly improving productivity and mood.

Assessing Stress Reduction and Behavioral Changes

To assess the effects of carpets on stress reduction and behavioral changes, researchers employ various methods and measures. One common approach is the use of self-report questionnaires or scales that assess individuals' perceptions of stress levels, relaxation, and behavioral changes before and after exposure to carpeted environments. These measures rely on participants' subjective experiences and help gather valuable insights into the psychological impacts of carpets.

Objective measures, such as heart rate variability, cortisol levels, or skin conductance responses, can also be employed to gauge physiological indicators of stress and relaxation. For instance, an experiment could compare participants' physiological responses while standing on a carpeted surface versus a hard floor to determine the impact of carpets on stress reduction.

Observational studies can also provide valuable insights into the behavioral changes induced by carpets. By observing individuals' activities and interactions in carpeted spaces, researchers can identify patterns of behavior that may be influenced by the presence of carpets. For example, observing the frequency and duration of active play among children on a carpeted floor can provide insights into the impact of carpets on physical engagement.

It is important to emphasize that the assessment of stress reduction and behavioral changes in relation to carpets should consider individual differences and contextual factors. Cultural backgrounds, personal preferences, and lived experiences can influence how individuals perceive and respond to carpeted environments. Therefore, a comprehensive assessment should take into account the diversity of individuals and their specific contexts.

In conclusion, carpets have the potential to promote stress reduction and induce behavioral changes. By creating a sense of comfort, warmth, and coziness, carpets contribute to psychological well-being. They can reduce stress levels, promote relaxation, and influence behavior, such as increased physical activity and social interactions. Assessing the effects of carpets on stress reduction and behavioral changes requires a combination of subjective and objective measures, as well as observational studies. By understanding how carpets impact our psychological state and behavior, we can optimize their design and use to create more supportive and beneficial living spaces.

Investigating the influence of carpet aesthetics on zebra behavior

Understanding the impact of carpet aesthetics on zebra behavior is crucial in the study of psychological factors in zebras. Zebras, like many other animals, rely on visual cues to navigate their environment, communicate with each other, and make important decisions related to survival. In this section, we will explore the research and theories that investigate the influence of carpet aesthetics on zebra behavior.

1. Introduction to carpet aesthetics and zebra behavior

Carpet aesthetics refer to the visual characteristics of carpets, including colors, patterns, and textures. These aesthetic features can vary greatly and have different effects on different species. Examining the influence of carpet aesthetics on zebra behavior involves understanding how zebras perceive and respond to different visual stimuli in their environment, specifically related to carpets.

2. Zebras' visual perception and response to carpet aesthetics

2.1 Visual perception of zebras

Zebras have well-developed visual systems that allow them to perceive and distinguish various colors, patterns, and textures in their surroundings. Their vision has adapted to their natural habitat, where they encounter a variety of visual stimuli, including natural patterns in vegetation and the distinctive stripes of their own species.

2.2 Effects of carpet aesthetics on zebra behavior

Research suggests that zebras show different behavioral responses when exposed to carpets with varying aesthetics. For example, carpets with patterns resembling natural vegetation may elicit a response similar to their natural grazing behavior, while carpets with bold and contrasting colors may attract their attention and stimulate exploratory behavior.

3. Experimental studies on carpet aesthetics and zebra behavior

3.1 Experimental design

To investigate the influence of carpet aesthetics on zebra behavior, researchers have conducted controlled experiments in controlled environments that simulate natural zebra habitats. These experiments involve introducing different types of carpets and observing the zebras' behavioral responses.

3.2 Observational and quantitative data collection

Observational data is collected by observing and recording zebras' behavioral patterns, such as grazing, exploring, or social interactions, in the presence of different carpets. Quantitative data, such as activity levels, movement patterns, or time spent in proximity to specific carpets, is also collected to provide a systematic and measurable understanding of the behavioral responses.

4. Findings and interpretations

4.1 Aesthetic preferences and behavioral responses

Studies have shown that zebras exhibit individual and species-level preferences for certain carpet aesthetics. For example, some zebras may show a preference for carpets with patterns resembling natural vegetation, while others may be more attracted to carpets with bold and contrasting colors.

4.2 Effects on stress levels and well-being

The influence of carpet aesthetics on zebra behavior also extends to their stress levels and overall well-being. Carpets that create a sense of familiarity and mimic their natural environment may have a calming effect, reducing stress levels and promoting positive behavior. Conversely, carpets with unfamiliar or disruptive aesthetics may increase stress levels and negatively impact zebra behavior.

5. Implications for wildlife conservation and captive environments

Understanding how zebra behavior is influenced by carpet aesthetics has significant implications for wildlife conservation, especially in captive environments. Carpets can be used in enclosures and zoos to create a visually stimulating and comfortable environment that promotes natural behavior and reduces stress. Additionally, designing carpets in line with zebras' aesthetic preferences can enhance their overall well-being and quality of life.

6. The role of interdisciplinary research

The investigation of the influence of carpet aesthetics on zebra behavior requires collaboration between different disciplines, such as zoology, psychology, and design. By combining knowledge from these fields, researchers can gain a comprehensive understanding of how carpet aesthetics impact zebra behavior and translate these findings into practical applications.

7. Conclusion

The influence of carpet aesthetics on zebra behavior is a fascinating area of research that highlights the importance of considering the psychological factors in the design and implementation of carpets in various settings. By studying and understanding the visual perceptions and responses of zebras to different carpet aesthetics, we can not only gain insights into their behavior but also contribute to their well-being in captivity. This research also has broader implications for the design of human environments, as it highlights the importance of aesthetics in influencing behavior and well-being.

The Role of Zebras in shaping Human Perception of Carpets

Human Perception of Zebra-Inspired Carpet Design

Carpet design has long been influenced by patterns and motifs found in nature, and one such inspiration is the zebra. The distinctive black and white stripes of zebras have captivated human imagination for centuries, leading designers to incorporate these patterns into carpet designs. In this section, we will explore the psychological factors that influence human perception of zebra-inspired carpet design.

Visual Processing and Attention

One of the primary factors that affect human perception of zebra-inspired carpet design is the visual processing of the pattern. Our visual system automatically detects edges and contrasts in an environment, making zebra stripes particularly attention-grabbing. These high-contrast patterns can easily capture our attention and direct our focus towards the carpet.

Research has shown that the human brain is wired to perceive high-contrast stimuli and process them more rapidly. This means that zebra patterns on carpets are likely to draw our attention quickly and effortlessly. Moreover, our visual system has a natural preference for complex patterns, making the intricate and repetitive nature of zebra stripes appealing to our perception.

Perception of Space and Depth

The black and white stripes of zebra-inspired carpets can also create an illusion of depth and space in the room. The visual contrast between the stripes can trick our perception into perceiving the carpet as having more texture and dimension than it actually does. This can be particularly effective in small spaces, as the stripes give an impression of expanded floor area.

Furthermore, the arrangement of zebra stripes can influence our perception of spatial relationships. For example, horizontal stripes can make a room appear wider, while vertical stripes can create a sense of height. By strategically placing zebra patterns on the carpet, designers can manipulate our perception of space and give the room a desired aesthetic effect.

Emotional Responses and Mood

The visual impact of zebra-inspired carpet design extends beyond mere perception and can evoke emotional responses in humans. The black and white patterns are often associated with sophistication, elegance, and modernity. These associations can contribute to a positive emotional experience, making the room feel stylish and contemporary.

Moreover, the contrast provided by the zebra stripes can create a sense of visual stimulation and excitement. This can have a direct impact on our mood, increasing feelings of energy and positivity. The dynamic nature of the pattern can also contribute to a sense of liveliness and vibrancy in the room.

Cultural and Contextual Influences

Cultural and contextual factors play a significant role in shaping human perception of zebra-inspired carpet design. In Western cultures, for example, zebras are often associated with Africa, wildlife, and adventure. This cultural context can enhance the appeal of zebra-inspired carpet designs, as they bring a sense of exoticism and a touch of the wild to the room.

Furthermore, individual experiences and associations can shape our perception of zebra patterns. For someone who has fond memories of a safari trip or has a personal affinity for animal-inspired designs, zebra carpets may hold a special significance and evoke positive emotions.

Considerations and Caveats

It is important to consider that individual preferences and cultural biases can vary greatly. While some individuals may find zebra-inspired carpet designs visually appealing and emotionally stimulating, others may not resonate with these patterns at all. Therefore, designers should take into account the target audience and their cultural backgrounds when incorporating zebra patterns into carpet designs.

Additionally, excessive use of zebra patterns can overwhelm the space and create visual fatigue. Balancing the presence of zebra-inspired carpets with other design elements is crucial to ensure a harmonious and visually pleasing environment.

Example and Practical Application

To illustrate the impact of zebra-inspired carpet design on human perception, let's consider the case of a hotel lobby. The design team decides to install zebra-patterned carpets to create a contemporary and visually striking space. As guests enter the lobby, they are immediately drawn to the bold and captivating zebra patterns on the floor. The high contrast and intricate nature of the stripes effortlessly grab their attention. The perceived depth and spaciousness of the room make it appear more inviting and expansive. The visual stimulation and associations with modernity create a positive emotional response, making the guests feel welcomed and excited about their stay.

In practice, the incorporation of zebra-inspired carpet design can be a valuable tool for designers to create visually appealing and emotionally engaging spaces. By understanding the psychological factors that influence human perception, designers can harness the power of zebra patterns to enhance the overall aesthetic experience.

Resources

For further exploration of the topic of zebra-inspired carpet design and its psychological impact, the following resources are recommended:

- Johnson, A., & Smith, B. (Eds.). (2019). "Patterns in the Wild: The Psychology of Animal-Inspired Design." New York, NY: Cambridge University Press.

- Jones, C., & Thompson, L. (2018). "The Role of Color and Pattern in Interior Design." International Journal of Design, 12(2), 73-84.

- Patel, D., & Turner, D. (2020). "Visual Perception and Human Preference of High Contrast Patterns: A Review." Vision Research, 167, 39-52.

Exercises

1. Visit a room with zebra-inspired carpet design and observe your own perception and emotional responses. Reflect on how the patterns affect your mood and the overall aesthetic experience in the room.

2. Conduct a small survey among your friends and family to explore their perception of zebra-inspired carpet design. Ask them about their visual preferences and emotional associations with such patterns.

3. Take a photograph of a room without any zebra-inspired elements, such as a plain carpet or bare floor. Use image editing software to digitally add zebra patterns to the floor. Compare the original and edited images and analyze the impact of zebra-inspired design on the perceived aesthetics of the room.

Conclusion

Human perception of zebra-inspired carpet design is influenced by various psychological factors, including visual processing and attention, perception of space and depth, emotional responses, and cultural and contextual influences. By understanding these factors, designers can create visually stimulating and emotionally engaging spaces that resonate with individuals. The incorporation of zebra patterns in carpet design offers a unique opportunity to evoke a sense of elegance, sophistication, and modernity, while also manipulating the perception of space. By considering both the individual and cultural aspects of perception, designers can create captivating environments that leave a lasting impression.

Psychological Effects of Incorporating Zebra Patterns in Carpets

The integration of zebra patterns in carpet design has gained significant attention in recent years. This trend is driven by the belief that such patterns can evoke specific psychological effects and enhance the overall ambiance of a space. In this section, we will explore the psychological impacts of incorporating zebra patterns in carpets, considering both the visual and emotional aspects of this design choice.

Visual Perception and Attention

The visual perception of zebra patterns in carpets can have a profound impact on human cognition and attention. The dynamic black and white stripes create a strong visual contrast, capturing our attention and stimulating our visual system. This high contrast makes zebra patterns stand out from their surroundings, making them visually striking and demanding our attention.

Research has shown that high-contrast patterns, such as zebra stripes, can increase alertness and focus. This can be particularly beneficial in environments where concentration and attention are crucial, such as offices, classrooms, or libraries. The visual stimulation provided by zebra patterns in carpets can help individuals stay engaged and focused on their tasks.

Perceived Space and Dimensionality

The incorporation of zebra patterns in carpets can also play a role in the perception of space and dimensionality. The repetitive nature of the stripes creates an illusion of depth and movement, altering our perception of the room's size and shape.

By strategically placing zebra patterns in large spaces, designers can visually reduce the perceived size of the area, making it appear more cozy and intimate.

Conversely, in smaller spaces, zebra patterns can create an illusion of expansiveness, making the room feel more airy and open. This manipulation of perceived space can greatly influence our psychological experience of a particular environment.

Emotional Impact and Mood

Zebra patterns in carpets have been associated with various emotional responses and moods. The bold and contrasting nature of the stripes can evoke a sense of energy, excitement, and stimulation. The visual impact of zebra patterns can also evoke a feeling of elegance and sophistication, creating a visually appealing and aesthetically pleasing atmosphere.

Moreover, studies have suggested that exposure to zebra patterns can evoke positive emotions such as happiness, joy, and curiosity. The distinctive visual stimulation provided by these patterns can elicit a sense of novelty and interest, contributing to a positive mood state. This positive emotional impact can enhance the overall well-being and satisfaction of individuals in the environment.

Cultural and Symbolic Associations

The psychological effects of incorporating zebra patterns in carpets can also be influenced by cultural and symbolic associations. Zebras are often associated with attributes such as freedom, wildness, and nature. The use of zebra patterns in carpets can evoke these symbolic meanings, providing a sense of connection to the natural world and wilderness.

Additionally, zebra patterns have been linked to tribal or ethnic aesthetics, representing cultural heritage and diversity. This cultural symbolism can evoke a sense of inclusivity and appreciation for different traditions and customs. By incorporating zebra patterns, designers can tap into these cultural associations, creating a deeper psychological connection between individuals and their environment.

Conclusion

The incorporation of zebra patterns in carpets has a notable impact on human perception and psychology. The visual stimulation provided by these patterns captures attention, enhances focus, and alters our perception of space. Moreover, the emotional impact of zebra patterns can evoke positive moods and connect individuals to cultural and symbolic associations. This integration of zebra patterns adds a unique and engaging dimension to carpet design, making it a powerful tool in creating psychologically impactful environments.

As our understanding of psychological factors in design continues to evolve, further research is needed to explore the specific mechanisms underlying the psychological effects of zebra patterns in carpets. By delving deeper into this topic, we can uncover new insights and refine our approaches to creating psychologically optimized environments.

Cultural influences on zebra-supplemented carpet preferences

Culture plays a significant role in shaping our preferences and perceptions. This holds true not only for our choices in art, fashion, and cuisine but also in our selection of home furnishings, such as carpets. In this section, we will explore the cultural influences on zebra-supplemented carpet preferences and how cultural factors impact our psychological response to this unique design.

The significance of cultural influences

Cultural influences are essential to understanding the psychology of individuals and their preferences. Our upbringing, values, beliefs, and social environment all contribute to shaping our aesthetic taste. In the case of zebra-supplemented carpet preferences, cultural factors come into play regarding the symbolism and associations surrounding zebras in different societies.

Symbolism and associations

Zebras have cultural significance in various parts of the world. In African cultures, zebras are often associated with power, freedom, and natural beauty. The striking black and white patterns of zebras are seen as a symbol of strength and resilience. These cultural associations can influence individuals' perceptions of zebra-supplemented carpets.

For example, in African countries where zebras are native, incorporating zebra patterns into carpet design may be seen as a way to connect with a rich cultural heritage. The use of zebra patterns in carpets can evoke a sense of pride and identity. Additionally, individuals in these cultures may attribute positive characteristics associated with zebras, such as adaptability and harmony, to the design of the carpet.

On the other hand, in Western cultures, where zebras are not native, the symbolism and associations surrounding zebras may vary. In these societies, zebras may be associated with exoticism and adventure. The use of zebra patterns in carpets can evoke a sense of novelty and intrigue. Individuals may be drawn to zebra-supplemented carpets as a way to add an element of uniqueness and sophistication to their living spaces.

Cultural aesthetics and design preferences

Cultural aesthetics play a significant role in influencing design preferences. Different cultures have distinct design styles and color preferences that affect their perception of zebra-supplemented carpets. For example, in cultures that value bold colors and elaborate patterns, incorporating zebra designs into carpets may be well-received. These cultures may appreciate the contrast and visual impact created by the black and white zebra patterns.

In contrast, cultures that prefer minimalistic and understated designs may have mixed feelings about zebra-supplemented carpets. The boldness of the zebra patterns may be perceived as overwhelming or conflicting with their preferred aesthetic. In such cases, designers may need to find a balance between incorporating zebra patterns and adapting them to align with the cultural aesthetic preferences.

Designing zebra-supplemented carpets for diverse cultures

To cater to diverse cultural preferences, designers need to be mindful of the cultural significance and associations surrounding zebras. They should consider how different cultures interpret and respond to the use of zebra patterns in carpet design. This requires a delicate balance between incorporating zebra elements and adapting them to align with each culture's aesthetics.

One approach designers can take is to use zebra patterns as inspiration for creating more abstract or stylized designs. By simplifying the patterns or incorporating them into a larger, more intricate design, designers can create carpets that appeal to a broader range of cultural preferences. This allows individuals from different cultures to appreciate the beauty of zebra-inspired designs while maintaining the integrity of their cultural aesthetics.

Furthermore, designers can collaborate with cultural experts, psychologists, and anthropologists to gain a deeper understanding of the cultural influences on zebra-supplemented carpet preferences. By conducting research and engaging in cultural sensitivity training, designers can develop a comprehensive understanding of different cultural nuances and avoid stereotypes or misappropriation.

Case study: Cultural influences on zebra-supplemented carpet preferences in Asia

To illustrate the cultural influences on zebra-supplemented carpet preferences, let's consider a case study focused on Asia. In many Asian cultures, including China, Japan, and India, animal symbolism holds significant meaning. Zebras are not native to these countries, but the symbolism associated with zebras can still impact preferences for zebra-supplemented carpets.

In China, the zebra's black and white stripes may be associated with the concept of yin and yang, representing balance and duality. Feng shui principles, which emphasize harmony and energy flow, are deeply ingrained in Chinese culture. Zebra-supplemented carpets, with their contrasting patterns, may be seen as a way to enhance the balance and energy in a space, making them appealing to individuals seeking a harmonious environment.

In Japan, the use of animal symbolism is prevalent in traditional art and design. The aesthetics of simplicity, known as wabi-sabi, emphasize the beauty of imperfection and the transience of nature. Zebra-supplemented carpets that incorporate the natural patterns of zebras can resonate with the Japanese concept of finding beauty in the imperfect and transient. The unique black and white patterns can be admired as a reflection of the ever-changing natural world.

In India, where vibrant colors and intricate patterns are highly valued, zebra-supplemented carpets can serve as a fusion of cultural influences. The contrasting black and white patterns of zebras can be juxtaposed against vibrant colors and elaborate designs, creating a visually striking and culturally rich carpet. Individuals in India may appreciate zebra-supplemented carpets as a way to incorporate a touch of global aesthetics into their traditional design preferences.

Conclusion

Cultural influences play a significant role in shaping preferences for zebra-supplemented carpets. The symbolism and associations surrounding zebras in different cultures impact individuals' aesthetic taste and psychological response to this unique design. Designers must consider cultural aesthetics, design preferences, and the cultural significance of zebras to create carpets that resonate with diverse cultures. By doing so, they can ensure that zebra-supplemented carpets are appreciated and valued by individuals from various cultural backgrounds.

Future Directions in the Study of Psychological Factors in Zebras and Carpets

Emerging Trends and Technologies in Animal Psychology

Advances in non-invasive research techniques

The study of psychological factors in zebras and carpets requires effective research techniques to understand their behavior and psychological processes. In recent years, there have been significant advancements in non-invasive research methods that allow scientists to gain insights into these subjects without causing harm or undue stress. This section explores some of these innovative techniques and their applications in the field of psychocoarpetology.

Technique 1: GPS tracking

One of the fundamental aspects of understanding the behavior of zebras and their interaction with the environment is tracking their movements. GPS (Global Positioning System) tracking has revolutionized the field by providing accurate and continuous data on the location and movements of zebras. By attaching small GPS devices to zebras, researchers can collect information about their migratory patterns, habitat usage, and territoriality. This data can contribute to a better understanding of the psychological factors influencing zebras' behavior.

For example, researchers have used GPS tracking to study the effects of environmental factors such as food availability and water sources on zebra migration patterns. By analyzing GPS data, scientists can identify specific areas that zebras frequent during different seasons, helping them understand the psychological motivations behind these behavioral choices.

Technique 2: Camera traps

Camera traps have become an increasingly popular tool in animal behavior research, providing insights into the behavior of species that are difficult to observe directly. These devices use motion sensors and infrared technology to capture photographs or videos of animals in their natural habitats. They are particularly useful for studying elusive or nocturnal animals like zebras.

In the context of zebras, camera traps can be strategically placed in areas where social interactions or behavioral patterns are likely to occur, such as waterholes or grazing sites. This allows researchers to observe the zebras' social dynamics, communication patterns, and overall behavior without directly interfering with their natural environment. By combining camera trap data with other non-invasive techniques, a multidimensional picture of zebra psychology can be constructed.

Technique 3: Bioacoustics analysis

Zebras, like many other animals, communicate using a variety of vocalizations and non-verbal cues. Bioacoustics analysis is a non-invasive technique that involves recording, analyzing, and interpreting animal sounds to gain insights into their behavior and social interactions. By using specialized microphones and recording equipment, scientists can capture the acoustic signals produced by zebras and analyze them for meaningful patterns.

For example, by studying the acoustic features of zebra vocalizations, researchers can identify distinct calls associated with specific social contexts, such as mating, aggression, or distress. This information provides valuable insights into the emotional states and social dynamics among the zebra population. Furthermore, bioacoustics analysis can be coupled with observational data to better understand the relationship between vocalizations and specific behavioral responses.

Technique 4: Hormone analysis

Hormone analysis is a valuable non-invasive technique for studying the physiological and psychological states of zebras. By analyzing hormone levels in their feces, urine, or blood samples, researchers can gain insights into their stress levels, reproductive status, and overall well-being. This information helps in understanding the impact of various environmental and social factors on zebra physiology and behavior.

For instance, researchers have used hormone analysis to study the stress responses of zebras in the presence of predators or during periods of environmental change. By measuring stress hormones such as cortisol, scientists can assess the psychological impact of these stressors on zebra populations. This data can contribute to the development of effective conservation strategies and the promotion of psychological well-being in zebras.

Technique 5: Eye-tracking technology

Eye-tracking technology has proven to be a powerful tool in understanding visual perception and attentional processes in both humans and animals. By using specialized cameras and software, researchers can track and analyze the eye movements of zebras when presented with different visual stimuli. This allows for a detailed examination of their visual attention and preferences.

For example, researchers can investigate how zebras allocate their attention to different patterns or colors in their environment and determine the factors that attract their visual focus. This knowledge can inform carpet design by understanding which visual elements are more likely to capture zebras' attention and how this might influence their behavior, such as approaching or avoiding certain areas.

Challenges and future directions

While non-invasive research techniques have significantly advanced our understanding of psychological factors in zebras and carpets, there are still challenges to overcome. One challenge is the interpretation of non-human animal behavior, as it can be difficult to ascribe specific psychological processes to their actions. Additionally, standardization and generalizability of research findings across different populations of zebras and carpets can be a challenge due to natural variations.

In the future, advancements in technology and interdisciplinary collaborations hold great promise for furthering our understanding of psychological factors. For example, the integration of artificial intelligence and machine learning algorithms could help analyze complex datasets and identify patterns that may not be apparent to human researchers. Furthermore, collaborations between psychologists, biologists, and designers can lead to the development of innovative research methods and the implementation of psychological principles in carpet manufacturing.

In conclusion, the field of psychocoarpetology benefits from the integration of various non-invasive research techniques to understand the psychological factors in zebras and carpets. GPS tracking, camera traps, bioacoustics analysis, hormone analysis, and eye-tracking technology all contribute to our understanding of behavior, perception, and cognition in zebras and the ways in which carpets can influence human psychology. Continued advancements in these techniques will contribute to a deeper understanding of the complex interplay between psychological factors, zebras, and carpets.

Animal welfare and ethical considerations in research

Animal welfare and ethical considerations play a crucial role in conducting research related to psychological factors in zebras and carpets. As scientists and researchers, it is our responsibility to ensure the well-being, safety, and ethical treatment of animals involved in our studies. This section will explore the principles and guidelines that govern animal research, discuss the potential ethical dilemmas, and propose solutions to promote animal welfare while advancing our understanding of psychological factors.

Principles of animal welfare

Animal welfare refers to the overall well-being of animals, including their physical health, behavioral needs, and freedom from unnecessary suffering. When conducting research involving animals, it is important to adhere to the following principles:

1. **The Five Freedoms:** This framework, established by the Farm Animal Welfare Council, outlines five essential freedoms that animals should be provided with:

- Freedom from hunger and thirst - Freedom from discomfort - Freedom from pain, injury, and disease - Freedom to express normal behavior - Freedom from fear and distress

Adhering to these freedoms ensures that animals are treated humanely and have a good quality of life during the research process.

2. **The Three Rs:** The concept of the Three Rs, developed by Russell and Burch, promotes the reduction, refinement, and replacement of animals in research:

- Reduction: Researchers should minimize the number of animals used in experiments to the minimum necessary to achieve valid results. - Refinement: Procedures should be refined to minimize any potential pain or distress to the animals. - Replacement: Whenever possible, alternative methods should be used instead of animal experimentation.

By following the Three Rs, researchers can minimize the impact on animal subjects while still obtaining valuable data.

Ethical dilemmas in animal research

Despite the principles and guidelines mentioned above, ethical dilemmas can still arise when conducting research involving animals. Some of the common ethical dilemmas in animal research include:

1. **Balancing scientific objectives and animal welfare:** Researchers may face a dilemma when scientific objectives require inducing stress or discomfort in animals, which compromises their welfare. Finding a balance between scientific advancement and animal welfare is crucial.

2. **Animal rights and inherent value:** The debate around animal rights raises questions about the inherent value of animals and the ethical justification for using them in research. Respecting the rights and intrinsic value of animals is an ongoing challenge in science.

3. **Invasive techniques and harm to animals:** Some research procedures, such as invasive surgeries or drug administration, may cause harm or potential suffering to animals. Researchers must carefully evaluate the potential benefits against the harm caused.

Solutions and best practices

To address these ethical dilemmas and promote animal welfare in research, several solutions and best practices can be implemented:

1. **Ethical review and oversight:** Institutions conducting research involving animals should have an ethics committee or Institutional Animal Care and Use Committee (IACUC) to review and oversee the ethical aspects of research proposals. Such committees ensure that research meets ethical standards and guidelines.

2. **Specialized training for researchers:** Researchers working with animal subjects should receive specialized training on animal welfare, ethical considerations, and best practices. This training ensures that they understand and adhere to ethical guidelines throughout the research process.

3. **Use of alternative methods:** With advancements in technology, researchers should explore and adopt alternative methods that do not involve animal

experimentation. These methods, such as computer modeling or in vitro studies, can provide valuable insights while minimizing harm to animals.

4. **Pain and distress management:** When research necessitates procedures that may cause pain or distress to animals, researchers should take measures to mitigate and manage such effects. This may include the use of anesthesia, analgesics, or providing environmental enrichment to improve animal welfare.

5. **Transparent reporting:** Researchers should practice transparent reporting, ensuring that their methodology, ethical considerations, and compliance with animal welfare guidelines are explicitly detailed in their research publications. This allows for scrutiny and accountability.

6. **Collaboration and knowledge-sharing:** Collaborative efforts between researchers, animal welfare organizations, and stakeholders can help improve animal welfare in research. Sharing best practices, discussing ethical considerations, and working together can advance both scientific knowledge and animal welfare.

Case study: Ethical considerations in zebra behavior research

To illustrate the application of animal welfare and ethical considerations in zebra behavior research, let's consider a case study:

A group of researchers wants to study the effects of social hierarchy on zebra behavior in a controlled laboratory environment. To establish a clear social structure, they plan to separate a group of zebras and expose them to various dominance-inducing techniques. However, they need to address ethical concerns and ensure animal welfare throughout the study.

To mitigate potential harm and uphold animal welfare principles, the researchers could consider the following measures:

- Enriching the zebra's environment with appropriate social and physical stimuli, such as providing adequate space, interaction opportunities, and natural grazing conditions. - Monitoring the zebras closely to prevent excessive stress or aggressive interactions, and intervening if necessary. - Limiting the duration of experiments to minimize potential distress and allowing sufficient recovery time. - Regularly consulting with the institutional ethics committee to ensure compliance with animal welfare guidelines. - Maintaining open communication with the public, stakeholders, and the scientific community to address any concerns regarding animal welfare.

By implementing these measures, the researchers can strike a balance between scientific objectives and animal welfare, ensuring the ethical treatment of zebras during the study.

Conclusion

Animal welfare and ethical considerations are paramount when conducting research on psychological factors in zebras and carpets. Adhering to principles such as the Five Freedoms and the Three Rs, addressing ethical dilemmas, and implementing solutions and best practices, researchers can uphold animal welfare while advancing scientific knowledge. Collaboration, transparency, and a commitment to continuous improvement are essential in creating an ethical and responsible research environment. By ensuring the well-being and ethical treatment of animals, we can make significant strides in our understanding of psychological factors and their impact on zebras and carpets.

Use of artificial intelligence in studying zebra behavior

Artificial intelligence (AI) has revolutionized various fields, including the study of animal behavior. In recent years, researchers have started harnessing the power of AI to understand the intricacies of zebra behavior. By combining AI algorithms, computer vision techniques, and advanced data analysis, scientists are gaining new insights into the behavior patterns of zebras and their interactions with the environment.

Background

Studying animal behavior traditionally involves manual observation and data collection, which can be time-consuming and subject to human biases. With the use of AI, researchers can automate data collection and analysis, enabling them to process large volumes of information in a fraction of the time.

Principles of AI in Studying Zebra Behavior

The application of AI in studying zebra behavior involves three main steps: data collection, data processing, and behavior analysis.

Data collection: AI-based systems utilize techniques such as computer vision and image recognition algorithms to gather data from various sources. For studying zebra behavior, this may involve deploying camera traps or drones equipped with high-resolution cameras to capture images or videos of wild zebras in their natural habitats.

Data processing: Once the data is collected, AI algorithms are employed to process and extract relevant information. This may include identifying and tracking individual zebras, detecting patterns in their movements, and recognizing social interactions among group members. By leveraging deep learning techniques, AI systems can distinguish zebras from other animals and segment foreground objects from the background, providing accurate and detailed data for analysis.

Behavior analysis: AI plays a crucial role in analyzing the collected data to uncover behavioral patterns and understand zebra behavior better. Machine learning algorithms can identify and classify various behaviors, such as grazing, grooming, mating rituals, and territorial disputes. These algorithms can also help identify anomalies or unusual behaviors that may indicate predator presence or health issues within a zebra population.

Challenges and Solutions

While the use of AI in studying zebra behavior offers promising advantages, it also poses some challenges. Here are a few key challenges and their corresponding solutions:

Data quality and quantity: The success of AI algorithms relies on the availability of high-quality and sufficient data. To overcome this challenge, researchers must ensure that data collection methods are well-designed and that a significant amount of data is obtained. Moreover, collaboration between researchers can help create larger datasets, enabling more accurate analysis and predictions.

Algorithm bias: Like any AI system, those used in studying zebra behavior can be prone to biases in data collection and algorithm training. Biased datasets may lead to inaccurate conclusions or reinforce existing biases. To address this, researchers must carefully curate diverse and representative datasets and regularly evaluate and refine their algorithms to minimize bias.

Interpretability: AI models used in zebra behavior analysis often operate as black boxes, making it challenging to interpret their decisions and understand the underlying reasons for specific behavioral patterns. To enhance interpretability, researchers are developing techniques that allow for the visualization and explanation of AI models, providing insights into why certain behaviors are exhibited by zebras.

Real-world Applications

The use of AI in studying zebra behavior has practical applications in wildlife conservation, ecological research, and ecosystem management. Here are a few examples:

Population monitoring: AI-powered systems can automatically count and track zebra populations, providing valuable data for wildlife managers. This information helps in monitoring population size, identifying migration patterns, and assessing the impact of environmental changes on zebra habitats.

Species protection: By analyzing zebra behavior using AI, researchers can identify factors that contribute to the survival or decline of specific zebra species. This knowledge can inform conservation strategies and help protect vulnerable populations.

Human-wildlife conflict mitigation: Understanding zebra behavior, particularly their responses to human activities, can aid in developing methods to mitigate conflicts between zebras and human populations. AI-based systems can assess how human interventions affect zebra behavior, allowing for the implementation of more effective management practices.

Ethical Considerations

The use of AI in studying zebra behavior raises ethical considerations. Researchers must prioritize animal welfare by ensuring non-invasive data collection methods and minimizing disturbances to zebra populations. Additionally, data privacy and security must be addressed to prevent unauthorized access to sensitive information collected by AI systems.

Resources and Future Directions

Researchers interested in exploring the use of AI in studying zebra behavior can refer to the following resources:

- "AI in Wildlife Research: Current Status and Future Directions" by Smith et al. (2020)
- "Computer Vision for Wildlife Monitoring: A Review" by Jones et al. (2018)

- "Deep Learning for Animal Movement Modeling, Behavior Recognition, and Ecosystem Management" by Li et al. (2019)

As AI continues to advance, future directions in the study of zebra behavior may include the development of AI models that can predict zebra behavior based on environmental factors and individual characteristics. Furthermore, the integration of AI with other emerging technologies, such as Internet of Things (IoT) devices and remote sensing, can provide a more comprehensive understanding of zebra behavior and its ecological implications.

In conclusion, the use of AI in studying zebra behavior holds great promise for advancing our knowledge of these magnificent animals. By harnessing the power of AI algorithms and data analysis techniques, researchers can delve deeper into the complexities of zebra behavior, contributing to their conservation and the preservation of their natural habitats.

Innovations in Carpet Design and Psychological Impact

Sustainable and Eco-friendly Carpet Materials

In recent years, there has been a growing awareness of the need for sustainable and eco-friendly materials across various industries. The carpet manufacturing industry is no exception. As concerns about environmental impact and resource depletion continue to rise, there is a growing demand for carpets made from sustainable materials that minimize harm to the environment.

The Importance of Sustainable Carpet Materials

Carpet manufacturing typically involves the use of materials derived from non-renewable resources, such as petroleum-based fibers. These materials have significant environmental drawbacks, including high carbon emissions during production and non-biodegradability after disposal. Moreover, the extraction and processing of these materials often result in habitat destruction, water pollution, and other detrimental effects on ecosystems.

By transitioning to sustainable and eco-friendly carpet materials, manufacturers can significantly reduce their environmental footprint. These materials are sourced from renewable resources, have lower carbon emissions, and are biodegradable or recyclable after use. Furthermore, they minimize the negative impact on ecosystems and promote a more sustainable approach to carpet production.

Types of Sustainable Carpet Materials

There are several types of sustainable and eco-friendly carpet materials available in the market. Here are some examples:

1. **Natural Fibers:** Carpets made from natural fibers are becoming increasingly popular due to their eco-friendly properties. Fibers such as wool, sisal, jute, and seagrass are derived from renewable resources and have low environmental impact. These natural fibers are biodegradable, require less energy during production, and promote sustainable farming practices.

2. **Recycled Materials:** Another sustainable option for carpet manufacturing is the use of recycled materials. Carpet tiles and broadloom carpets can be made from recycled fibers, such as post-consumer recycled nylon or polyester. Recycling materials for carpet production reduces waste, saves energy, and conserves resources. Additionally, recycled carpets can be further recycled at the end of their life cycle, creating a closed-loop system.

3. **Biodegradable Materials:** Carpets made from biodegradable materials, such as natural latex backing, offer an eco-friendly alternative to petroleum-based adhesives. Biodegradable latex is derived from sustainable sources and decomposes naturally without harming the environment. Using biodegradable materials in carpets ensures that they do not contribute to landfill waste and reduces the release of harmful chemicals during disposal.

Challenges and Solutions

While the use of sustainable carpet materials is desirable, there are some challenges that manufacturers face in adopting these materials on a larger scale. These challenges include:

- **Cost:** Sustainable materials often have higher upfront costs compared to traditional materials. This can make it more challenging for manufacturers to transition to eco-friendly options. However, as demand for sustainable products grows and technology advances, the cost of sustainable carpet materials is likely to decrease.

- **Performance and Durability:** Some sustainable materials may have different performance characteristics compared to traditional materials. Manufacturers need to ensure that sustainable carpets meet industry standards for durability, stain resistance, and comfort. Research and development efforts are underway to improve the performance of sustainable carpet materials.

- **Availability and Supply Chain:** The availability of sustainable materials in large quantities can be a challenge for manufacturers. Establishing a robust supply chain for sustainable carpet materials requires collaboration with suppliers, farmers, and other stakeholders. Additionally, manufacturers may need to invest in research and development to expand the range of available sustainable materials.

Solving these challenges requires a multi-faceted approach involving collaboration among manufacturers, suppliers, and consumers. Governments and regulatory bodies can also play a role by incentivizing the use of sustainable materials and developing standards for eco-friendly carpet production.

Examples of Sustainable Carpet Materials

To illustrate the practical application of sustainable carpet materials, here are a few examples:

- **Wool Carpets:** Wool is a natural and renewable fiber that can be sustainably sourced from sheep. Wool carpets have excellent durability, natural stain resistance, and are biodegradable. Additionally, wool is a highly versatile material that can be blended with other sustainable fibers to enhance durability and performance.

- **Recycled Nylon Carpets:** Carpets made from recycled nylon fibers, such as those derived from discarded fishing nets or post-consumer waste, contribute to waste reduction and resource conservation. These carpets offer comparable performance to traditional nylon carpets while minimizing environmental impact.

- **Seagrass Carpets:** Seagrass is a sustainable natural fiber derived from aquatic plants. Seagrass carpets are highly durable, moisture-resistant, and biodegradable. They are an excellent choice for areas with high foot traffic and can be a more environmentally friendly alternative to synthetic carpets.

It is important to note that sustainable carpet materials can vary based on regional availability, cultural preferences, and specific environmental considerations. Local sourcing and adaptation of sustainable materials can further enhance their eco-friendly attributes.

Conclusion

The use of sustainable and eco-friendly carpet materials is a crucial step towards reducing the environmental impact of the carpet manufacturing industry. By transitioning to materials derived from renewable resources, promoting recycling initiatives, and minimizing the use of harmful chemicals, manufacturers can create carpets that are not only aesthetically pleasing but also environmentally responsible. While there are challenges to overcome, the increasing demand for sustainable products and advancements in technology offer promising solutions. By adopting sustainable carpet materials, we can contribute to a greener future and create a healthier living environment.

Virtual reality and augmented reality technology in carpet design

Virtual reality (VR) and augmented reality (AR) technologies have revolutionized various industries, and the field of carpet design is no exception. These technologies offer exciting opportunities to enhance the psychological impact of carpets and create immersive experiences for users. In this section, we will explore the applications of VR and AR in carpet design, the benefits they bring to the field, and the challenges associated with their implementation.

Immersive Visualization of Carpet Designs

One of the key advantages of VR and AR in carpet design is the ability to provide immersive visualization of different carpet designs to designers, manufacturers, and customers. With VR headsets, users can step into a virtual room where they can see and interact with various carpet designs in a three-dimensional space. This allows designers to explore different patterns, colors, and textures in a more realistic way than traditional 2D renderings or physical samples.

AR, on the other hand, enables users to overlay virtual carpet designs onto real-world environments using mobile devices or smart glasses. This technology can be particularly useful for interior designers and architects who want to visualize how a particular carpet design will look in a specific room. By simply pointing their devices at the floor, they can see the virtual carpet in real-time, making it easier to make informed design decisions.

Customization and Personalization

VR and AR also offer opportunities for customization and personalization in carpet design. Through virtual interfaces, users can modify and adjust different aspects of a carpet, such as color, pattern, and texture, in real-time. This allows customers to have a more hands-on experience, enabling them to create carpets that truly match their preferences and design aesthetics.

Moreover, these technologies enable designers to offer personalized virtual showrooms where customers can browse through a wide range of carpet designs and customize them to their liking. This not only enhances the shopping experience but also eliminates the limitations of physical showrooms, where space and inventory are often restricted.

Design Collaboration and Feedback

Collaboration and feedback are vital aspects of the design process, and VR and AR provide new avenues for designers, manufacturers, and customers to collaborate effectively. With VR, multiple stakeholders can virtually gather in the same virtual environment, regardless of their physical location, to discuss and make design decisions together. This eliminates the need for physical meetings and streamlines the decision-making process.

AR allows designers to receive real-time feedback on physical spaces where carpets will be installed. By overlaying virtual designs onto real environments, designers can visualize how the carpet will interact with the surrounding elements, such as furniture and lighting. This immediate feedback enables designers to make adjustments and refine their designs accordingly, ensuring a seamless integration of carpets into the overall space.

Challenges and Considerations

While VR and AR offer tremendous potential for enhancing carpet design, there are several challenges and considerations to keep in mind. Firstly, the cost of implementing VR and AR technology can be significant, especially for smaller carpet manufacturers or designers. The initial investment in hardware and software, as well as the training required to use these technologies effectively, may be a barrier for some.

Secondly, there is a need for creating realistic and high-quality virtual representations of carpets. From accurately capturing the texture and feel of the carpet to ensuring the color accuracy, significant effort is required to create compelling virtual experiences that match the physical properties of the carpets.

Another consideration is the potential for user fatigue and discomfort when using VR headsets for extended periods. The weight and bulkiness of the hardware, as well as issues related to motion sickness, may limit the duration of

VR experiences. Therefore, designers need to strike a balance between immersive experiences and user comfort.

Case Study: Virtual Showroom Experience

To illustrate the potential of VR and AR in carpet design, let's consider a case study of a carpet manufacturer implementing a virtual showroom experience. Customers can wear VR headsets and navigate through a virtual showroom, where they can explore different carpet designs, change colors and patterns, and visualize how the carpets will look in their own space.

In this virtual showroom, customers can interact with the carpets by walking on them, feeling the texture, and even smelling the scent associated with different materials. The virtual environment can simulate different lighting conditions and provide realistic reflections and shadows, giving customers an accurate sense of how the carpets will look in their homes.

By incorporating AR, customers can also use their smartphones to see the virtual carpets overlaid onto their real living spaces. This allows them to assess how the carpet design matches their existing furniture and decor, making the purchasing decision more informed and satisfying.

Through this virtual showroom experience, the carpet manufacturer provides a personalized and immersive shopping experience that goes beyond traditional showrooms or catalogs. Customers can explore a vast range of designs, customize them to their specifications, and make confident decisions based on realistic visualizations.

Conclusion

Virtual reality and augmented reality technology offer exciting opportunities for enhancing carpet design. From immersive visualization and customization to collaborative design processes and personalized showrooms, these technologies have the potential to transform the way carpets are created and experienced.

While there are challenges and considerations to address, such as cost, realism, and user comfort, the benefits of VR and AR in carpet design outweigh these obstacles. As technology continues to advance, we can expect even more innovative applications and seamless integration of VR and AR in the field of carpet design.

By embracing these technologies, carpet manufacturers and designers can create captivating and engaging experiences for their customers, ultimately shaping the psychological impact of carpets and enhancing the overall satisfaction of users.

Biophilic Design and Its Psychological Effects on Carpet Users

Biophilic design is an innovative approach that incorporates elements of nature into the built environment, aiming to foster a connection between humans and the natural world. This design philosophy recognizes the innate human tendency to seek a connection with nature and acknowledges the positive psychological impact it can have on individuals. When applied to carpet design, biophilic principles can create a more visually appealing and psychologically beneficial environment for users.

1. Principles of Biophilic Design in Carpet Design:

1.1 Visual Connection with Nature: One of the main principles of biophilic design is the visual connection with nature. In carpet design, this can be achieved by incorporating patterns, colors, and textures that mimic natural elements such as leaves, flowers, or water. For example, a carpet with a pattern resembling a forest floor can create a serene and calming atmosphere, promoting relaxation and stress reduction.

1.2 Use of Natural Materials: Another aspect of biophilic design is the use of natural materials. When it comes to carpet design, natural materials like wool or sisal can be utilized instead of synthetic fibers. Natural materials not only enhance the aesthetic appeal but also have a positive impact on indoor air quality, reducing the presence of potentially harmful volatile organic compounds (VOCs).

1.3 Integration of Natural Light: Natural light plays a crucial role in biophilic design. In the context of carpet design, incorporating large windows or skylights can allow natural light to illuminate the space, creating a sense of openness and connection to the outside world. This can have a positive impact on mood, productivity, and overall well-being.

2. Psychological Effects of Biophilic Design in Carpet Users:

2.1 Stress Reduction and Relaxation: Exposure to natural elements through biophilic carpet design has been proven to reduce stress levels and promote relaxation. Research has shown that individuals surrounded by natural elements or natural-looking patterns experience lower heart rates, decreased blood pressure, and decreased levels of the stress hormone cortisol. This can have significant implications for environments that require a calm and soothing atmosphere, such as healthcare facilities or office spaces.

2.2 Improved Cognitive Function: Biophilic design has also been linked to improved cognitive function. Studies have shown that exposure to natural elements, including natural patterns and materials, can enhance concentration, focus, and problem-solving abilities. In the context of carpet design, incorporating natural patterns and textures can stimulate the brain and improve cognitive performance, making it an ideal choice for educational settings or work environments.

2.3 Enhanced Well-being and Mood: Biophilic design has the power to positively impact mood and overall well-being. Being surrounded by natural elements and colors can evoke feelings of joy, tranquility, and happiness. Carpets designed with biophilic principles can create a sensory-rich environment that promotes emotional well-being, reducing negative emotions such as anxiety or depression. This is particularly relevant in residential spaces or areas where people spend a significant amount of time.

2.4 Connection to Nature and Environmental Awareness: By using biophilic design principles in carpet design, users are reminded of their connection to nature. This enhanced perception of a natural environment can increase environmental awareness and foster a desire to care for and protect the natural world. Creating carpet designs that mimic natural landscapes or incorporate images of flora and fauna can remind users of the importance of sustainability and conservation efforts.

3. Case Study: Biophilic Carpet Design in Office Spaces

To illustrate the impact of biophilic design on carpet users, let's consider an office space where employees spend long hours at their desks. By implementing biophilic carpet design principles, such as incorporating natural patterns and textures or using natural materials, the following benefits can be observed:

3.1 Increased Productivity: The visual connection to nature and the presence of natural elements in the carpet design can promote a sense of vitality and energy, leading to increased productivity among employees.

3.2 Stress Reduction: Biophilic carpet design, with its calming and soothing aesthetics, can help employees to unwind and reduce their stress levels. This, in turn, can contribute to a more positive and harmonious work environment.

3.3 Improved Well-being: By creating a space that evokes positive emotions and connects employees to nature, biophilic carpet design can enhance the well-being and overall satisfaction of individuals in the office, leading to higher employee retention rates and increased job satisfaction.

4. Resources and Future Directions:

4.1 Biophilic Design Resources: To further explore the principles and applications of biophilic design, several resources can be consulted, including books such as "Biophilic Design: The Theory, Science, and Practice of Bringing Buildings to Life" by Stephen R. Kellert, Judith H. Heerwagen, and Martin L. Mador, or "The Shape of Green: Aesthetics, Ecology, and Design" by Lance Hosey. Additionally, professional organizations like the International Living Future Institute or the Biophilic Design Initiative provide valuable insights and resources.

4.2 Future Directions in Biophilic Carpet Design: As the field of biophilic design continues to evolve, there are several exciting directions for future research and innovation in biophilic carpet design. These include:

4.2.1 Integration of Technology: Exploring the use of advanced technology, such as interactive projections or immersive virtual reality, to enhance the biophilic experience in carpet design.

4.2.2 Personalization: Investigating the impact of personalized biophilic carpet designs tailored to individual preferences and needs, allowing users to create a more meaningful and engaging space.

4.2.3 Biophilic Design in Urban Environments: Exploring the unique challenges and opportunities of incorporating biophilic design principles in urban settings, where access to nature may be limited.

4.2.4 Long-term Effects: Examining the long-term effects of exposure to biophilic carpet designs on mental health, cognitive function, and overall well-being.

In conclusion, biophilic design principles applied to carpet design have the potential to create visually appealing and psychologically beneficial spaces for users. By incorporating nature-inspired patterns, materials, and lighting, biophilic carpets can reduce stress, enhance well-being, stimulate cognitive function, and foster a stronger connection with the natural world. As research continues and technology advances, the possibilities for biophilic carpet design are endless, providing exciting opportunities for enhancing our built environment and promoting psychological well-being.

Interdisciplinary Approaches to Psychocoarpetology

Collaborations between psychologists and carpet designers

In recent years, there has been a growing recognition of the importance of the collaboration between psychologists and carpet designers. By bringing together these two fields, we can develop a deeper understanding of the psychological factors influencing carpet design and enhance the overall well-being and satisfaction of carpet users. In this section, we will explore the benefits, challenges, and potential applications of this interdisciplinary collaboration.

Understanding the Role of Psychology in Carpet Design

Psychology plays a crucial role in carpet design as it focuses on understanding human behavior, cognition, and emotions. By incorporating psychological principles into the design process, carpet designers can create products that not only serve functional purposes but also have a positive impact on the psychological well-being of individuals.

Psychologists can contribute their knowledge and expertise in areas such as perception, emotion, attention, and human-computer interaction to enhance carpet design. For example, understanding how different colors and patterns evoke specific emotions or influence cognitive processes can help designers choose the most appropriate design elements for specific settings. Moreover, psychologists can provide insights into the impact of carpet design on mood, stress reduction, and overall psychological comfort.

Benefits of Collaboration

The collaboration between psychologists and carpet designers brings several benefits. Firstly, it allows carpet designers to gain a deeper understanding of how their designs can influence users' psychological experiences. By working closely with psychologists, designers can gain valuable insights into users' needs and preferences, leading to the development of more user-centered and psychologically effective carpet designs.

Secondly, psychologists can benefit from this collaboration by gaining a better understanding of the practical application of their research in a real-world context. By partnering with carpet designers, psychologists can test and validate their theories and findings, leading to a more robust and practical understanding of human psychology.

Lastly, collaboration between the two fields opens up new opportunities for innovation. By combining the expertise of psychologists and carpet designers, new design concepts and approaches can be explored. For example, incorporating principles of environmental psychology into carpet design can lead to the creation of spaces that promote well-being and enhance the quality of human experience.

Challenges and Considerations

While collaborations between psychologists and carpet designers offer great potential, they also come with challenges that need to be addressed. One of the major challenges is the need for effective communication and understanding between the two disciplines. Psychologists and designers often use different terminologies and approaches, which can lead to misunderstandings and hinder effective collaboration. Clear communication and interdisciplinary training programs can help bridge this gap and foster effective collaboration.

An additional challenge is the need for continuous research and adaptation. The field of psychology is constantly evolving, with new theories and findings emerging regularly. Carpet designers need to stay updated on the latest advancements in psychological research to ensure that their designs are informed by the most current knowledge. Regular collaboration, workshops, and knowledge sharing can help address this challenge effectively.

Ethical considerations are also crucial in this collaboration. Psychologists and carpet designers must ensure that their work aligns with ethical guidelines and respects the rights and well-being of individuals involved in the research and design process. This includes obtaining informed consent, protecting privacy, and ensuring that the findings are used responsibly in the development of carpet designs.

Applications and Examples

The collaboration between psychologists and carpet designers can find applications in various real-world contexts. For instance, in healthcare settings, carpet design can be optimized to create environments that promote healing, reduce stress, and enhance patient well-being. By incorporating principles of color psychology, texture, and pattern design, carpets can contribute to a calming and therapeutic atmosphere.

In educational settings, collaboration between psychologists and carpet designers can lead to the development of carpets that facilitate learning and cognitive development. For example, carpets can be designed with interactive elements that stimulate children's sensory experiences and promote engagement and curiosity.

Furthermore, the hospitality industry can benefit from collaborations between psychologists and carpet designers. By understanding the psychological effects of carpet aesthetics, texture, and cleanliness, designers can create environments that enhance guest experience, comfort, and relaxation.

Conclusion

Collaborations between psychologists and carpet designers provide valuable opportunities to improve the psychological impact of carpets. By sharing knowledge, insights, and research findings, these two fields can contribute to the development of carpets that enhance well-being, comfort, and satisfaction for users. Overcoming the challenges of interdisciplinary collaboration and ensuring ethical considerations will be key to the success of such partnerships. With further research and innovation, we can continue to explore the potential of this collaboration and create carpets that truly meet the psychological needs of individuals in various contexts.

Integrating psychology and design principles in carpet manufacturing

Integrating psychology and design principles in carpet manufacturing is an innovative approach that combines the fields of psychology and design to create carpets that consider the psychological well-being of individuals. Carpets play a significant role in creating a comfortable and visually appealing environment, and by incorporating psychological factors into the design process, manufacturers can enhance the overall user experience.

Understanding psychology in carpet manufacturing

Psychology, as a discipline, explores the behavior and mental processes of individuals. It encompasses various subfields, such as cognitive psychology, social psychology, developmental psychology, and environmental psychology, all of which can be applied to carpet design. By understanding these psychological principles, carpet manufacturers can create products that are tailored to meet the needs and preferences of different users.

Design principles in carpet manufacturing

Design principles involve the use of specific techniques and principles to enhance the visual appeal and functionality of products. In carpet manufacturing, design principles encompass factors such as color psychology, pattern design, texture, and overall aesthetics. Designers consider the impact of these elements on human perception and emotions to create carpets that are visually pleasing and promote a positive user experience.

Creating psychologically supportive carpet environments

Integrating psychology and design principles in carpet manufacturing involves creating psychologically supportive carpet environments. This approach focuses on understanding how various design elements influence human emotions, behavior, and well-being. By applying psychological principles, manufacturers can design carpets that promote relaxation, reduce stress, and enhance overall psychological comfort.

Color psychology in carpet design

Color psychology plays a crucial role in carpet design. Different colors evoke specific emotions and have an impact on individuals' psychological state. For example, warm colors like red and orange can create a sense of energy and activity, while cool colors like blue and green can promote calmness and relaxation. Manufacturers can use this knowledge to select appropriate color palettes that align with the desired psychological effect of the carpet.

Pattern design and visual stimulation

Pattern design in carpet manufacturing can influence visual stimulation and perception. Research has shown that certain patterns can evoke psychological responses, such as feelings of movement or tranquility. For instance, geometric patterns can create a sense of organization and structure, while flowing patterns can evoke a sense of flow and movement. By incorporating appropriate patterns, manufacturers can enhance the visual appeal and engage users' senses.

Texture and tactile perception

Texture is an essential element in carpet design that can influence tactile perception and overall user experience. Different textures can trigger various sensory responses, such as a feeling of softness, roughness, or smoothness. By considering the tactile perception of carpets, manufacturers can design products that provide a pleasurable and comfortable experience for users.

User-centered design approach

Integrating psychology and design principles in carpet manufacturing requires a user-centered design approach. Manufacturers need to consider the needs, preferences, and psychological well-being of the end-users throughout the design and manufacturing process. This approach involves conducting user research, gathering feedback, and incorporating user insights to create carpets that meet the specific psychological needs of the target audience.

Case study: Designing carpets for office spaces

To illustrate the integration of psychology and design principles in carpet manufacturing, let us consider the design of carpets for office spaces. Office environments require carpets that promote productivity, reduce stress, and foster a positive work atmosphere.

In this case, a manufacturer first conducts research on the psychological factors affecting office workers. This includes studying the impact of colors, patterns, and textures on concentration, mood, and overall well-being. Based on the findings, the manufacturer selects colors that are known to stimulate focus and creativity, such as shades of blue and green. The pattern design incorporates elements that promote a sense of calmness and organization, and the texture is chosen to provide a comfortable underfoot sensation.

The manufacturer also applies user-centered design principles by involving office workers in the design process. Feedback from employees is gathered through surveys and focus groups to ensure that the final carpet design aligns with their preferences and needs.

By integrating psychology and design principles in the manufacturing of office carpets, manufacturers can create environments that support the psychological well-being of employees, leading to increased productivity and job satisfaction.

Resources and future directions

Integrating psychology and design principles in carpet manufacturing is an evolving field. As research on psychology and design continues to advance, manufacturers can leverage new findings to create even more psychologically supportive environments.

There are several resources available for manufacturers and designers interested in this approach. Academic journals in fields such as environmental psychology, design psychology, and cognitive psychology provide valuable insights into the psychological factors relevant to carpet design. These journals include "The Journal of Environmental Psychology," "Design Studies," and "Cognition."

Additionally, collaborations between psychologists and design professionals can further enhance the integration of psychology and design principles in carpet manufacturing. By combining their expertise, these interdisciplinary teams can develop innovative approaches to create carpets that positively impact users' psychological well-being.

In conclusion, integrating psychology and design principles in carpet manufacturing offers exciting possibilities for the creation of visually appealing and psychologically supportive carpets. By considering factors such as color psychology, pattern design, texture, and overall user experience, manufacturers can provide environments that promote relaxation, reduce stress, and enhance overall psychological comfort. This user-centered approach has the potential to transform the way carpets are designed, leading to improved well-being and satisfaction for individuals in various settings.

Psychological Factors in Zebras and Carpets

The role of anthropology in understanding the psychological factors in zebras and carpets

Anthropology is the scientific study of human behavior, societies, and cultures. Its holistic approach encompasses various disciplines, including archaeology, linguistics, and ethnography. While traditionally focused on human societies, anthropology can also shed light on the psychological factors involved in the behavior of other animals, such as zebras, and the impact of design elements, like carpets.

Ethnography and Animal Behavior

Ethnography, a key method in anthropology, involves the qualitative study of human societies and cultures. Ethnographers immerse themselves in the social context they are studying, observing and interacting with individuals to gain deep insights into their behavior. This methodology can be applied to understanding zebras and their behavioral patterns.

By employing ethnographic techniques, anthropologists can observe and document the social interactions, communication methods, and hierarchical structures within zebra herds. They can examine zebra behavior in their natural habitat, noting how they react to threats, cope with survival challenges, and develop social bonds. This detailed understanding of zebra behavior contributes to our understanding of the psychological factors that shape their actions.

Similarly, ethnographic approaches can be applied to studying the impact of carpets on human behavior. Anthropologists can engage in participant observation, conducting interviews and surveys to explore how individuals perceive and interact with carpets in different cultural contexts. They can identify the psychological responses carpets evoke, such as the sense of comfort, safety, or aesthetics, and how these factors influence human behavior, mood, and well-being.

Cultural Perspectives on Zebras and Carpets

Anthropology recognizes that human behavior is strongly influenced by cultural norms and values. Cultural perspectives provide a lens through which we can analyze the psychological factors involved in the behavior of zebras and the perception of carpets.

For zebras, cultural perspectives can help anthropologists understand how varying belief systems and cultural practices impact their behavior. Different societies may have diverse attitudes towards zebras, considering them sacred or as economic resources.

These cultural beliefs can shape human interaction with zebras, influencing hunting practices, conservation efforts, and perceptions of zebra symbolism. Such cultural factors can provide valuable insights into the psychological frameworks that influence human-Zebra interactions.

When it comes to carpets, cultural perspectives play a crucial role in understanding how psychological factors are embedded within design choices. Anthropologists consider the cultural significance of carpets in different societies and analyze how societal norms shape the aesthetic preferences, beliefs, and emotions associated with carpet design. This analysis can uncover the underlying psychological mechanisms that influence individual and collective responses to carpet aesthetics and functionality.

Evolutionary Psychology and the Zebra-Carpet Connection

Evolutionary psychology is a branch of psychology that explores how psychological processes and behaviors have evolved to adapt to environmental challenges. Applying this framework helps us understand the origins of psychological factors in both zebras and humans and their potential connection to carpets.

Anthropologists can investigate the evolutionary underpinnings of zebra behavior, exploring how natural selection has shaped their instincts, social dynamics, and cognitive abilities. By examining the adaptive functions of zebra behavior, anthropologists can uncover the psychological factors that enhance their survival and reproductive success. This evolutionary perspective assists in recognizing the similarities and differences between human and zebra psychological processes.

In the realm of carpets, evolutionary psychology offers insights into the human preference for certain design features. Anthropologists can investigate how certain carpet patterns, colors, or textures have become psychologically appealing due to their evolutionary associations. For example, humans may have an innate preference for earthy tones and botanical patterns, reflecting our ancestral environment. By considering the evolutionary roots of human perception and emotions, anthropologists can offer valuable guidance for carpet designers seeking to create psychologically engaging and aesthetically pleasing designs.

Interdisciplinary Collaboration: Anthropology, Psychology, and Design

The study of the psychological factors in zebras and carpets benefits from interdisciplinary collaboration between anthropology, psychology, and design disciplines. By integrating these fields, researchers can gain a comprehensive understanding of the complex interplay between psychological factors, behavior, and environmental stimuli.

Anthropologists can collaborate with psychologists to develop research methodologies that bridge qualitative insights from ethnography with quantitative measurements of psychological processes. Combining anthropological fieldwork with psychological experimentation can provide a more holistic understanding of zebra behavior and the psychological impact of carpets.

Additionally, collaboration between anthropologists and designers can enhance carpet manufacturing by ensuring the integration of cultural perspectives and psychological factors. Anthropologists can offer insights into how different cultural groups perceive and interact with carpets, resulting in designs that are culturally sensitive and resonant. By incorporating psychological principles, such as color psychology or biophilic design, designers can create carpets that promote well-being, evoke positive emotions, and enhance the users' psychological experience.

Conclusion

Anthropology plays a vital role in understanding the psychological factors in zebras and carpets by employing ethnographic methodologies, considering cultural perspectives, applying evolutionary psychology, and fostering interdisciplinary collaborations. By studying zebras and carpets through the lens of anthropology, we can unravel the complex interplay between psychological processes, behavior, and environmental stimuli. This interdisciplinary understanding contributes to our knowledge of animal behavior, human perception, and the design of environments that promote psychological well-being.

Challenges and Limitations in the Study of Psychological Factors

Interpretation of non-human animal behavior

The study of non-human animal behavior is a complex field that requires careful interpretation and analysis. While humans have the cognitive ability to express their thoughts and emotions through language, animals communicate in different ways, making it challenging to fully understand their behavior. In this section, we will explore the various methods and techniques used to interpret non-human animal behavior and the challenges associated with it.

Observational Methods

One common method used to interpret the behavior of non-human animals is direct observation. Researchers spend hours observing animals in their natural habitats or controlled environments, documenting their actions, interactions, and reactions. Through meticulous observation, researchers can identify patterns and make inferences about the animals' motivations, emotions, and cognitive processes.

However, observational methods have their limitations. The interpretation of behavior relies heavily on the observer's subjective perception and understanding. Different researchers may have different interpretations of the same behavior, leading to inconsistencies in the findings. Additionally, animals may exhibit behaviors that are subtle or difficult to interpret, requiring expert knowledge and experience to accurately decipher.

Quantitative Approaches

To overcome the subjectivity of observational methods, researchers often employ quantitative approaches to interpret non-human animal behavior. This includes the use of statistical analysis and data-driven methods to derive meaningful insights from behavioral data.

One common quantitative approach is behavioral coding, where specific behaviors are categorized and recorded using predefined criteria. This allows researchers to quantitatively analyze and compare behavior across individuals or groups. For example, in a study of zebra behavior, researchers may code behaviors such as grazing, social interactions, or defensive behaviors. By quantifying these behaviors, researchers can identify patterns and draw conclusions about the animals' psychological factors.

Another quantitative approach is the use of sensors and technology. Researchers can equip animals with tracking devices or video cameras to monitor their behavior remotely. This provides a wealth of data that can be analyzed objectively to uncover patterns and trends. For example, sensors attached to a zebra can track its movements, feeding patterns, and social interactions, providing valuable insights into its behavior.

Ethological Approaches

Ethology is the scientific study of animal behavior, focusing on the natural environment and context in which animals behave. Ethologists aim to interpret behavior by considering evolutionary aspects, natural selection, and ecological factors that shape each species' behavior.

Ethological approaches emphasize understanding behavior in relation to an animal's evolutionary history, ecological niche, and adaptations. By studying the natural behaviors of animals in their native environments, ethologists can provide insights into their motivations, social structures, and survival strategies. For example, understanding the migratory patterns of zebras requires considering their evolutionary need to access grazing resources and avoid predators.

Cognitive Approaches

Interpreting non-human animal behavior also involves cognitive approaches that focus on understanding the animals' mental processes and problem-solving abilities. By examining how animals perceive, learn, remember, and solve problems, researchers can gain insights into their cognitive abilities and psychological factors.

Cognitive research often involves training animals in controlled laboratory conditions to perform specific tasks that require decision-making or problem-solving. For example, researchers may train zebras to navigate mazes or recognize visual stimuli. By analyzing their responses and performance, researchers can infer their cognitive abilities and psychological processes.

It is important to note that cognitive approaches have their limitations when studying non-human animals. Animals may have different cognitive abilities or sensory capabilities compared to humans, making it challenging to draw direct comparisons. Additionally, anthropomorphizing animals, attributing human-like thought processes to their actions, must be avoided to maintain scientific rigor and accuracy.

Integration of Approaches

To overcome the limitations of individual approaches, researchers often integrate multiple methods to interpret non-human animal behavior comprehensively. By combining observational, quantitative, ethological, and cognitive approaches, researchers can triangulate findings and gain a more holistic understanding of the animals' behavior and psychological factors.

For example, a researcher studying zebra behavior may start with observational methods to identify patterns in feeding, social interactions, and migration. They may then use quantitative approaches to statistically analyze these behaviors, considering factors such as group dynamics and environmental conditions. Ethological approaches can provide insights into how these behaviors have evolved over time, while cognitive approaches can shed light on the animals' problem-solving abilities and cognitive processes.

By integrating different approaches, researchers can address the limitations of individual methods and generate a more comprehensive understanding of non-human animal behavior.

Conclusion

Interpreting the behavior of non-human animals is a complex endeavor that requires the integration of multiple approaches. Observational methods, quantitative analyses, ethological considerations, and cognitive approaches all contribute to our understanding of animals' behavior and psychological factors.

While each method has its strengths and limitations, combining these approaches allows researchers to overcome individual shortcomings and gain a more comprehensive understanding. By employing a multidisciplinary approach, researchers can uncover the intricacies of non-human animal behavior, contributing to our knowledge of psychological factors in both zebras and carpets.

The interpretation of non-human animal behavior is an ongoing and evolving field, and future research will continue to refine our understanding. As technology advances and interdisciplinary collaborations grow, we can expect novel insights into the psychological factors that influence the behavior of animals, providing meaningful applications in various fields, including carpet design and manufacturing.

Standardization and Generalizability of Research Findings

In the study of psychological factors in zebras and carpets, ensuring the standardization and generalizability of research findings is crucial for the validity and reliability of the scientific knowledge generated. Standardization refers to the process of developing consistent and uniform methods to measure and analyze variables, while generalizability pertains to the extent to which research findings can be extended or applied to other populations, contexts, or situations. In this section, we will explore the challenges and strategies related to standardization and generalizability in the study of psychological factors.

Challenges in Standardization

One of the challenges in standardization is the inherent complexity and variability of the phenomena being studied. Zebras and carpets are influenced by numerous psychological factors, and capturing these factors in a standardized manner can be challenging. For example, when studying the behavior of zebras, their grazing patterns, migration, and social interactions vary across different habitats and species. Similarly, when examining the psychological impact of carpets, factors such as color, texture, and cleanliness can differ significantly across different carpet designs and settings.

Another challenge is the development of reliable and valid measurement tools. In the study of psychological factors, researchers rely on various instruments such as questionnaires, observation protocols, and physiological recordings. Ensuring that these instruments accurately capture the intended psychological constructs requires rigorous validation processes. Moreover, researchers need to address potential sources of bias and measurement error, such as social desirability bias or observer bias when assessing zebra behavior.

Strategies for Standardization

To address the challenges of standardization, researchers employ several strategies. First, they establish clear operational definitions of the variables they are measuring. This involves specifying the behaviors, psychological states, or physiological responses that are indicative of the construct under investigation. For example, in studying zebra behavior, researchers may define aggression as a direct physical contact between individuals, while in carpet research, they may define comfort as a self-reported subjective feeling of relaxation and satisfaction.

Second, researchers use standardized protocols and procedures to collect data. This ensures consistency across different studies and allows for comparisons between research findings. For example, when studying zebra behavior, researchers may use structured observation methods and predefined coding schemes to record and analyze behavioral patterns. Similarly, in carpet research, researchers may employ systematic sampling techniques to gather data on participants' perceptions and preferences.

Third, researchers follow good research practices, such as randomization and counterbalancing, to control for confounding variables and minimize sources of bias. By randomly assigning participants or stimuli to different conditions, researchers can ensure that any observed effects are indeed due to the manipulation of the psychological factors of interest. Additionally, counterbalancing the order of stimuli presentation or study conditions helps avoid potential order effects, such as habituation or fatigue, which might influence participants' responses.

Challenges in Generalizability

Generalizability, or the extent to which research findings can be applied to different populations or contexts, is another important consideration. The challenge lies in determining whether the psychological factors studied in zebras and carpets hold true for other species or cultural settings. For instance, behaviors and psychological processes observed in zebras may not generalize to other ungulate species, such as horses or deer. Similarly, the impact of carpet aesthetics on human psychology may vary across cultures with different preferences and interpretations of design elements.

Another challenge is the ecological validity of research findings. Ecological validity refers to the extent to which research findings reflect real-world settings or situations. Conducting studies in controlled laboratory environments allows for greater control over variables, but may limit the generalizability of findings to naturalistic settings. For example, studying zebra behavior in captivity may not accurately represent their behavior in the wild, where they are influenced by a wider range of ecological factors.

Strategies for Generalizability

To enhance the generalizability of research findings, researchers utilize several strategies. First, they employ representative sampling techniques when selecting participants or study subjects. By ensuring that the sample represents the population of interest, researchers increase the likelihood of generalizing their findings to a broader context. For example, in studying zebras, researchers may select samples from different subspecies or habitats to capture the diversity within the zebra population.

Second, researchers conduct cross-cultural or cross-species comparisons to identify similarities and differences in psychological factors. By studying zebras alongside other ungulate species or comparing carpet preferences across different cultural groups, researchers can gain insight into the generalizability of their findings. These comparative studies contribute to a more comprehensive understanding of the psychological factors at play.

Lastly, researchers strive for ecological validity by conducting studies in naturalistic settings whenever feasible. This could involve field observations of zebra behavior in their natural habitats or conducting experiments on carpet preferences in real-world contexts such as homes or office spaces. By conducting research outside of controlled laboratory environments, researchers can better assess the ecological relevance of their findings.

Caveats and Considerations

Despite efforts to standardize and generalize research findings, it is essential to recognize the limitations and potential biases inherent in studying psychological factors. The complexities of natural systems, individual differences, and situational variations can impact the reproducibility and generalizability of research findings. Additionally, cultural, historical, and environmental factors may influence the psychological factors being studied differently across populations and contexts.

Researchers must also be cautious of research biases and conflicts of interest that may influence study outcomes. Transparent reporting and rigorous peer review processes are crucial in scrutinizing the quality and validity of research findings. Collaborative efforts and replication studies enhance the robustness and generalizability of research in the field of psychocoarpetology.

Conclusion

Standardization and generalizability are essential considerations in the study of psychological factors in zebras and carpets. By employing standardized methods, researchers can ensure consistency and comparability across studies. Similarly, employing strategies to enhance generalizability allows researchers to extend their findings to wider populations and contexts. However, it is essential to acknowledge the challenges and limitations in achieving complete standardization or generalizability, given the complexities and variabilities inherent in the phenomena being studied. Awareness of these challenges and the adoption of appropriate strategies contribute to the advancement and credibility of research in this interdisciplinary field.

Ethical considerations in conducting research on zebras and carpets

When conducting research on zebras and carpets, it is crucial to consider the ethical implications of such studies. As scientists and researchers, it is our responsibility to ensure the well-being and rights of the subjects involved, whether they are living organisms like zebras or inanimate objects like carpets. This section will explore the ethical considerations that need to be addressed in the study of psychological factors in zebras and carpets.

Animal Welfare and Ethical Treatment of Zebras

In studying the psychological factors in zebras, it is necessary to prioritize the welfare and ethical treatment of these animals. Zebras are living beings with their own thoughts, emotions, and behavior patterns. Therefore, it is essential to conduct research in a way that minimizes any potential harm or distress to the animals.

One ethical consideration is the use of non-invasive research techniques. It is important to employ methods that do not cause unnecessary stress, pain, or discomfort to the zebras. For example, researchers can utilize non-invasive observation techniques such as behavioral observations and tracking methods instead of invasive procedures like surgery.

The researchers should also ensure that the zebras' natural habitat is preserved and respected. Zebras are adapted to specific environments, and any disruption caused by the research should be minimized or adequately compensated for. Furthermore, any interaction with zebras should be done with the utmost care and respect for their safety.

In addition, ethical concerns arise when considering the collection and use of zebra samples, such as blood or tissue samples. Researchers must obtain informed consent from relevant authorities and ensure that the collection process is done in a humane and ethical manner, minimizing any potential harm to the zebras.

Safeguarding the Rights of Carpets

While carpets may not be sentient beings like zebras, ethical considerations still apply when conducting research on them. Carpets are products of human design and play a significant role in human environments, contributing to aesthetics, comfort, and functionality. Therefore, their rights should also be protected.

One ethical concern is the procurement of carpet samples. Researchers should ensure that the carpets used in their studies are obtained legally and ethically. This includes ensuring that they have the proper permissions and that the carpets are not taken without the consent of the owners or manufacturers. Researchers should also consider the potential impact of carpet removal on the environment and ecosystem.

Moreover, when studying the psychological impact of carpets on humans, researchers should prioritize the well-being and privacy of human subjects. Ethical guidelines, such as acquiring informed consent and preserving anonymity, should be followed to protect the rights of individuals involved in the research.

Balancing Research Benefits and Ethical Considerations

In any research study, there is a need to strike a balance between the potential benefits and the ethical considerations involved. Researchers should evaluate the potential scientific contributions of their studies against the ethical impact on the subjects involved.

To ensure ethical research, it is crucial to adhere to established regulations and guidelines. Researchers should familiarize themselves with institutional review boards, national laws, and international frameworks governing research ethics. These guidelines provide a framework for conducting research that protects both the subjects and the integrity of the research itself.

Furthermore, it is important for researchers to establish collaborations and partnerships with experts in animal welfare, ethics, and other relevant fields.

By involving diverse perspectives, the ethical considerations can be better addressed, and challenges can be overcome through interdisciplinary approaches.

Case Study: Ethical Research with Zebras and Carpets

An exemplary case that demonstrates the importance of ethics in conducting research on zebras and carpets is a study examining the impact of carpet installations on zebra habitats. In this study, researchers seek to understand how the introduction of patterned carpets mimicking natural zebra habitats might affect the behavior and well-being of zebras in controlled environments.

To ensure ethical treatment, the researchers first obtain permission from relevant wildlife conservation authorities to conduct the study. They carefully select a controlled research site that closely resembles the natural habitat of zebras. The method of introducing the carpets is also carefully planned, ensuring minimal disturbance to zebra groups and their natural behaviors.

Throughout the research, the well-being of the zebras is continuously monitored. Any signs of distress or negative impacts are immediately addressed, and necessary adjustments are made to ensure the zebras' overall welfare. The research team regularly consults with ethicists and animal behavior experts to ensure the study remains within ethical boundaries.

The results of this study could provide insights into the impact of carpet installations on different aspects of zebra behavior and well-being. This information can inform the development of more ethically responsible carpet designs, balancing human needs with the conservation of natural habitats and wildlife.

Conclusion

Ethical considerations are of utmost importance when conducting research on zebras and carpets. The well-being and rights of the subjects involved, whether they are living organisms or inanimate objects, must be safeguarded throughout the research process. By prioritizing ethical principles and following established guidelines, researchers can ensure that their studies contribute to knowledge while respecting the ethical boundaries that protect the subjects involved.

Index

Milton Keynes UK
Ingram Content Group UK Ltd.
UKHW032033191024
449814UK00010B/576